THE COMPLETE BOOK OF WILD BOAR HUNTING

THE COMPLETE BOOK OF WILD BOAR HUNTING

Tips and Tactics That Will Work Anywhere

BY TODD TRIPLETT

The Lyons Press
Guilford, Connecticut
An imprint of The Globe Pequot Press

Copyright © 2004 by Todd Triplett

ALL RIGHTS RESERVED. No part of this book may be reproduced or transmitted in any form by any means, electronic or mechanical, including photocopying and recording, or by any information storage and retrieval system, except as may be expressly permitted in writing from the publisher. Requests for permission should be addressed to The Lyons Press, Attn: Rights and Permissions Department, P.O. Box 480, Guilford, CT 06437

The Lyons Press is an imprint of The Globe Pequot Press.

Printed in the United Stated of America

10 9 8 7 6 5 4 3 2 1

ISBN: 1-59228-428-0

Library of Congress Cataloging-in-Publication Data is available on file.

DEDICATION

This book is dedicated to my best friend in the world, Sherry. She encourages me when the going gets tough and celebrates with me when I make it through. I hope we'll be able to chase hogs, deer, turkeys, and other game together for many years to come.

It goes without saying, but each time I enter the forest or field I feel God's presence all around me. I know of very few hunters, anglers, or outdoorsmen who don't feel the same way.

CONTENTS

INTRODUCTION 1
  1. The Wild Boar 9
  2. Hunting Methods 21
  3. Finding and Interpreting Sign 43
  4. Equipment 55
  5. Year-Round Hunting 73
  6. Southern Hogs 87
  7. Western Hogs 99
  8. Preserve Hunting 109
  9. Hunting Hogs Around the World 123
 10. Javelina 131
 11. Warthogs 145
 12. From Field to Table 157
 13. Trophy Preparation 171
 14. Tips for Successful Hunting 183
Appendix: Finding Places to Hunt Wild Boar 197
Index 205

INTRODUCTION

After hunting the last two hours before darkness fell, I began to make my way out of the forest. I traveled slowly, walking ten paces and then stopping to listen. As my flashlight was back at camp, only dim moonlight lit my path. My caution was prompted by a fear of too close an encounter with a wild hog. Meeting an old boar or, even worse, a sow with piglets wouldn't be much fun in the dark.

The sounds of wild hogs resonated throughout the Georgia island on which I was hunting. Grunts and squeals assured me I wasn't alone. The vocal hogs were fine; it was the thought of a silent one that bothered me. The hogs were plentiful and seemingly unthreatened by my presence. Even so, I didn't want to end up needing stitches that I could only get after a long ride out by truck and then boat.

Tales from old-timers who had extensive experience with wild hogs raced through my mind as I worked my way back to camp. "They're tougher'n a pine knot and equally as mean if ya get 'em riled." Or, "If a biggun runs by he'll usually be shakin' his head tryin' to getcha with his tusks." Though I had never had a close encounter with a wild hog, I didn't want to start now—at least not in the dark. At least in the daylight I would be able to quickly find a small tree to shinny up out of harm's way.

Nearly to the halfway mark, with almost a quarter-mile to go, I stopped again to listen. In the distance, I could hear leaves rustling and a hog grunting as he made his way toward me. As the

Black Beard's Island off the Georgia coast still appears much as it did when the first explorers released hogs here several hundred years ago. (Eric Smith)

hog closed the distance to less than fifty yards I could feel the hair on the back of my neck standing on end. All I could do was listen and try to gauge the distance between us. He came closer—forty yards, then thirty, twenty, ten. At ten yards, he stopped. Armed with only a bow, I didn't dare move. Even if I'd had a plan, I couldn't see well enough in the inky night to go anywhere fast.

The standoff lasted less than ten seconds. Luckily, the wind was quartering across my back, and the last thing the hog must have wanted was an encounter with a predator. With a grunt, he made a hasty retreat into the thicket. When the sounds of the scurrying hog finally faded I breathed a sigh of relief and continued toward camp.

The remainder of the hunt held its share of surprises, but nothing quite matched that encounter in the dark. One thing is for certain; I never forgot my flashlight again.

Introduction

That hunt took place off the coast of Georgia on a private island that is adjacent to well-known Black Beard's Island. Although hunted regularly, the hogs there were high in number and provided ample opportunities during the three-day hunt. I have heard tales of other private islands all along the southeastern coast that are also home to large populations of wild hogs. Once hogs establish themselves, they spread like wildfire, and we'll discuss the reasons for this in the pages ahead.

On another hunt in the lowlands of South Carolina, the action was equally as fast, but with a vastly different mood. We were using catch dogs to find and "bay" hogs, which is a common practice among hog hunters, especially in the Southeast. We had hunted most of the morning with little success, and it looked as

My son took his first hog on an island off the coast of Georgia.

3

though we might be in for a long day. After hood rigging a dog in a large parcel of property without any luck we decided to try a different location. Within five hundred yards of pulling onto the main road, a keeper-sized black hog crossed up ahead.

The hog headed into the same block of woods that we had permission to hunt, so we quickly pulled to the side of the road and released three eager hounds. They found the trail in short order, and the race was on. I gathered my archery equipment as quickly as possible. My hunting partner and I, along with the dogs' owner, began to follow the sweet sounds known only to those who have hunted with hounds.

After traveling less than three hundred yards, the stubborn hog bayed and began defending himself from the yapping, nipping dogs. Though less than half the weight of the hog, at around

This hound is more than ready to take on an oversized hog.

Introduction

sixty pounds each, the three hounds were able to force the hog into holding tight. This was no easy task, as the boar, with at least an inch of tusk protruding from each side of his mouth, desperately wanted to leave.

Because things can happen very quickly when hunting with hounds, we wasted no time setting up for a short shot. It's a tricky operation, as a swirling hog surrounded by three lunging hounds doesn't make the easiest target for a broadhead. We had to wait for just the right moment.

Our first concern was for the safety of everyone in the hunting party. And, of course, the hounds were part of our hunting party. All dog handlers know the value of a good hound and are understandably hesitant to risk harm to their hunting companions. So we had a couple options at this point: We could wait until a low-risk shot opportunity presented itself or we could call off the dogs. The latter is really only an option if the dogs are trained well enough to listen to their master despite the excitement and chaos.

Happily for us, these dogs were trained to retreat upon command. So with the hog in position for a good shot, the dog owner gave the hounds the command, "Back." Without hesitation, two hounds quickly retreated from the scene. But the third ... well, he had something else in mind. This was his hog—or so he thought—and come hell or high water he wasn't leaving. After a couple more commands without a response, the handler decided to take matters into his own hands and remind the dog about the meaning of the word "back."

As his owner drew closer, the hound became more aggressive toward the hog. The feisty hound must have been thinking either, "Look, Dad, I'll whip 'em all by myself" or "This hog will not get my master." The tension mounted like the last round of a boxing match as the handler closed to within mere feet of the hound. But we weren't prepared for what happened next.

Apparently, having the man and dog so close was more than the jet-black critter could take. The hog decided it was time to leave now or end up on the barbecue grate. Just as the owner reached for the dog's collar, the hog decided to make his break. Unfortunately for the hog, the only escape route was a narrow path just to one side of the dog, which now seemed to be in a state of total panic. The handler got his hand on the collar just as the hog bolted. But before the hog could squeeze through the only available opening, the hound lunged forward and clamped down on its ear.

Now, anyone who understands much about wildlife and hunting dogs knows that dogs are strong but hogs are stronger. And the handler, well, he evidently had just enough strength to keep a hold on the collar. The bizarre train of hog, dog, and handler held together for about ten feet before the inevitable happened. First, the handler came to his senses and released the hound, then the dog released his prize and the chase resumed. But the hog ran less than fifty yards before all three dogs once again surrounded him.

We again closed in for a shot. This time everything went as planned. The dogs kept the hog in position until we approached within easy bow range. Then, all three retreated at the handler's call. Already holding at full draw, I wasted no time in settling my pin a couple of inches behind the boar's front shoulder. The Muzzy broadhead passed completely through the hog, burying itself in the ground beyond.

Mortally wounded, the hog made another attempt to escape. He made it less than thirty yards before expiring, with the dogs on his tail the entire way.

Introduction

Silently, I paid my respects to the hog. He would provide food for family and friends, as well as a fond hunting memory for my hunting partner and me. Needless to say, I was certain the dog handler would remember this hunt as one of his wildest.

Most hog hunters have experienced similar circumstances to the ones related above at one time or another. Hog hunting is, for the most part, a very close, intense experience. Sure, some hogs are taken in excess of one or two hundred yards, but the majority are taken within bow range. Because of this, many hog hunters tote short-range weapons like bows, pistols, shotguns, or even knives or spears.

On the island referred to earlier, some areas were so thick I often couldn't see ten feet in front of me. The only way to hunt effectively in a situation like that is to get in a tree, which offers at least a limited view down into the thick foliage. As for hunting with hounds, it's not uncommon for a hunter or dog handler to have to get that close to a tusker. With the exception of the chain formed by hog, dog, and handler, most hunts that utilize dogs are quite similar.

Hog hunting is almost always an up-close-and-personal experience, which seems to be a major part of the attraction for many hunters.

WELCOME TO OUR WORLD

Welcome to the world of hog hunting. Some of my most memorable moments, knee slapping as well as hair raising, have occurred during hog hunts. Hogs have lagged well behind major big game species in popularity, but more hunters than ever are now taking to the field after this critter. The word is out that the hunts are incredibly exciting and that hog meat makes wonderful table fare. And though some states are attempting to completely eradicate hogs,

The Complete Book of Wild Boar Hunting

Because of the exciting action, liberal bag limits, and low cost, hog hunting can become very addictive. (Steve Smith)

others are embracing them as a major attraction for hunters, thus creating cash flow for rural communities in what would otherwise be the off-season.

Whether you hunt hogs in the East or West, on a preserve up north, or in the rolling hills of Texas, you'll find plenty of thrills. And if you've never hunted hogs at all, you're missing out on some of the best hunting around.

This book is filled with valuable hunting information and tips for beginner and experienced hog hunters alike. But it doesn't end there. Key hunting areas are also covered, along with tips for field care, trophy preparation, and even a few recipes.

Till we meet in the woods, remember my slogan, "Life is short, hunt hard!"

Chapter 1

THE WILD BOAR

Partly due to the lack of attention they receive from major sporting magazines, numerous fallacies persist about wild hogs and hunting them. One is the assumption that any hog that is black in color is from a pure Russian bloodline. While Russian boars—some more pure than others—do still exist, the majority of hogs killed in North America are of mixed blood. These crosses are between the Eurasian bloodline and the bloodlines of many other countries. The Eurasian strain included hogs from Ireland, Japan and, obviously, Russia. Other bloodlines originated in countries like Spain, Australia, and parts of South America.

HOW THEY GOT HERE

Hunting Russian boar enjoyed a long tradition in Eastern Europe before sport hunters brought the animals to North America in the late 1800s. And many other strains were introduced through domestic farm animals that escaped or were turned loose in the woods. These hogs are usually referred to as "feral," which basically just means wild. For serious hunters, dubbing any hog as feral is a way of separating it from a true Russian boar.

While mammals have been present in North America for thousands of years, the wild hog is a relative newcomer. Most historians agree that the first hogs, or pigs, if you will, were brought to our shores by the Spanish explorer Hernando De Soto in 1539. They landed in what is now Florida, which to this day remains a prime destination for hog hunters. His expedition eventually covered most of the Southeast.

Although it's less talked about, Polynesians also introduced hogs to the Hawaiian Islands as early as A.D. 1000.

Settlers took the pigs to both locations as a ready food supply. This is easy to understand, as most hogs have no predators other than man. And because they're omnivores they can virtually care for themselves. They'll feed on almost anything from tubers and grasses to carrion or bird eggs. This characteristic is what helped these tasty critters spread so quickly across nearly half the country.

Feral hogs are now found in approximately thirty states, although this number fluctuates a bit as hogs are eliminated from some areas or released in others. (These releases

Hogs introduced in the Southeast were from domestic stock that roamed free and became feral over time.

The Wild Boar

Feral hogs like this one are now found in nearly thirty states across the country. (California Department of Fish and Game)

are generally illegal, done without the knowledge of state fish and game departments.)

Because pigs needed very little care, they were allowed to move about freely. This practice was known as "free-roam farming," and it was very time and cost effective. Hog farmers would mark their pigs in some way, and then allow them to go wherever they wanted. As long as food was available, most hogs didn't go far.

When the farmers were ready to gather their hogs they formed roundups with neighboring farmers, similar to those performed in cattle country. Most of the hogs in an area would be herded into catch pens, where they were separated by their markings and claimed by the farmers. Those still too small to slaughter or sell were then released to continue to grow. Of course, many cagey hogs were never caught, and eventually their owners gave up on

The Complete Book of Wild Boar Hunting

Wild hogs come in many color phases with charcoal, or black, the most common. (Charlie Tanner)

them. *Voila!* After a few generations, these hogs became as wild as any animal on the continent.

Russian boars, on the other hand, were brought to this country by hunters seeking a prolific animal that provided good sport and table fare. These first hogs were evidently released into a 20,000-acre enclosure in the state of New Hampshire. It didn't take long for a few hogs to escape. They dug under the fences or trees fell on the fencing and opened up holes. The rest, as they say, is history.

While a few states still boast of having true Russian boars, it is highly unlikely these days. It's not impossible, of course,

Domestic hogs have a distinct appearance that distinguishes them from their wild cousins. These differences include larger ears, a corkscrew tail, and a stockier build. (California Department of Fish and Game)

The Wild Boar

just unlikely. However, many states and Canadian provinces are home to a fairly pure Eurasian hog. From my own observations, I can say that most bloodlines in the Southeast are far from pure anything, as this was the home turf of the original feral hogs.

RECOGNIZING DIFFERENCES

Regardless of the cross breeding that has taken place over the years, all wild hogs have traits that, by appearance, link them more closely to the bloodlines of pure Russian boars or domestic pigs. These differences are sometimes quite pronounced, but they're obviously fairly vague in animals that have crossbred extensively.

Russian boars have smaller ears but much longer snouts and legs than their domestic counterparts. Their tails are straight, and most have tufts at the tip. Hair color is light brown to coal black, and sometimes a cream or tan color is evident on the ends. Also, the hair along the center of the back is longer than on the remainder of the body. When the animal is frightened or excited these hairs can rise like hackles on a dog's back.

Wild boar can reach forty inches at the shoulder, and males can weigh up to 450 pounds. Females hold their

This hog, taken by a bowhunter in the Cumberland Mountains of Tennessee, exhibits traits characteristic of a pure Russian bloodline.

own, though, as weights up to nearly 400 pounds have been documented. A feral hog is usually a bit shorter at the shoulder, and may weigh as much as 300 pounds. But average weight for both Russian and feral hogs—boar or sow—is roughly 120 to 150 pounds, depending on habitat and genetics. Of course, there are also tall (true?) tales of monster hogs weighing 700 pounds or more.

OTHER CHARACTERISTICS

Wild boars and feral hogs are very intelligent animals, a trait that helps them adapt easily to new surroundings. This adaptation can include everything from successfully evading hunters to locating food sources in relatively lean years. The intelligence of domesticated and feral hogs has been studied extensively, and scientists have found that the only animal group with a higher intelligence level is the primates—orangutans, chimpanzees, etc.

As with any other species, there is a pecking order among wild hogs. This hierarchy isn't very noticeable, though, as most hogs aren't very aggressive toward one another beyond a small tussle now and then. Dominance more often takes the form of an adult pushing a youngster out of the way while feeding. More aggressive behavior only shows up when males battle over a sow in heat, and even then it's more like a light shoving match than an all-out brawl. Still, you'll find that most adult boars have a thick shield along each shoulder area that protects them against the tusks of their opponents.

Hogs tend to travel single file when moving from one feeding or bedding area to another. When they reach their destination, they usually disperse and go about their business until it's time to leave, at which point they form a line again and head out. Sows will take the lead most of the time, followed by the shoats, or piglets. If any boars are in the group, they'll take up a position at the back of the line—something hunters would do well to remember when scanning a group for the best animal to take.

In the first few weeks after the piglets are born, groups tend to include only the mother and her young. Then, as the young mature, boars and other family groups will join to form larger herds. The largest group I have ever seen at one time included around twenty-five hogs. These were mostly young animals, although I counted at least ten adults.

Wild hogs have an excellent sense of smell, and this is usually their first line of defense against hunters. They also hear very well, so stalking hunters must be particularly careful. A hog's eyes are important for detecting danger, but not as much as the nose and ears. Some hunters believe that wild hogs are nearly blind, and I must admit that in areas that aren't hunted extensively, and with an appropriate wind, I have been able to sneak within twenty yards of a group of feeding hogs. On the other hand, I have hunted areas that are heavily pressured only to find cautious hogs that easily pick out human silhouettes. Just like all wild animals, hogs are always alert for a variety of clues that might indicate danger.

NO CLOSED SEASON, NO BAG LIMITS

Within the United States, California, Texas, and Florida are the most widely known hog-hunting destinations, due in no small part to their extremely high populations of feral hogs. Many other states are home to very high numbers of hogs, and on a per-acre basis may have as many or more than the "big three" states. Oklahoma, Hawaii, South Carolina, Alabama, and Georgia are among the states that don't receive as much attention from hunters despite extremely high hog populations in certain areas.

Many hunters claim that New Hampshire, North Carolina, and areas within Texas are home to the largest populations of Russian boar with fairly pure bloodlines. In addition to well-documented populations, some areas aren't even on the charts because of shady importation and release practices by private parties.

Most states with resident hog populations have very liberal seasons and bag limits; in many states, there are no regulations at all. This can make for an exceptional off-season hunting experience.

These liberal or nonexistent bag limits are in place because hogs can wreak all kinds of havoc on habitat important to a wide range of other species. Hogs are notorious for rooting, which involves turning up the top layer of soil to find roots and tubers. This activity often destroys desirable native vegetation. Hogs also consume vast amounts of food that would otherwise be eaten by animals that are indigenous to the area.

And as hogs are very prolific, they will quickly reproduce to the point of overpopulation if not controlled by hunting. Under ideal conditions, a sow can breed up to three times annually, although the average sow will breed only twice. Most litters average six piglets, but up to ten are possible. That is a lot of hogs in a short period of time, which is why state wildlife biologists are usually anxious to keep numbers down.

DISEASE

As if all this destruction and overpopulation weren't enough, hogs can also bring disease to an area. Though the effects of these diseases are sometimes over-hyped, hogs do actually carry diseases that are harmful to wildlife, livestock, and, in rare cases, humans. The

The Wild Boar

Without regulation, hog numbers can soar, wreaking havoc on habitat. (California Department of Fish and Game)

two most common of these are pseudorabies and swine brucellosis, although hogs may also carry tuberculosis, anthrax, and tularemia.

Pseudorabies is a viral disease that can affect domestic and feral hogs, cattle, horses, goats, sheep, dogs, and cats. Signs include a loss of weight, excessive salivation, spasms, convulsions, and paralysis. Pseudorabies is in no way related to the rabies virus, and it does not infect humans.

Swine brucellosis can cause infertility in boars and abortions in sows. Therefore, it's mostly detrimental to hog farmers rather than the average hunter. However, this disease is transmittable to humans. Effects from this disease range from flu-like symptoms to arthritis and meningitis. Fortunately, it can be treated with antibiotics, although these treatments are costly and uncomfortable, to say the least.

Both diseases are of special concern to domestic hog owners, as they can lower and possibly eliminate reproduction. And once a hog contracts either disease, it's a carrier for life. If infected animals aren't found and disposed of quickly the disease will spread rapidly.

TROPHY STATUS

As with any other game animal, the trophy status of a wild boar depends on who is doing the judging. Do you want a hog that will provide the best eating? Is this your first hog? Do you simply want the largest hog possible? All hogs can be trophies, but in general a trophy animal will be an older, larger male with the longest possible tusks. Such a hog has outwitted predators and outlived his siblings through a higher level of intelligence and good genes.

Trophy status is usually determined by a combination of weight and tusk length. Though both can vary depending on habitat and genetics in a given area, most hog hunters agree that any animal that exceeds 150 pounds is definitely a trophy. And hogs that weigh in excess of 300 pounds are almost unheard of.

A good general guideline for trophy tusk length would be around one and a half to two inches, measured from the gum line. Larger tusks do occur, but it's uncommon. Both males and females have tusks, but a female's are very small and rarely extend past the lips. It usually takes at least four years for a boar to achieve maximum tusk length, so any animal with long tusks will also be an older, heavier male.

Tusks this length may not seem very large, but you must also consider the terrain in which a hog lives. If the habitat is rugged the tusks will often be broken, chipped, or worn down. In addition, the whets—the teeth directly above the tusks—are continually sharpening the tusks, which prohibit them from growing to excessive length. Sometimes, freaks of nature occur whose whets don't match

The Wild Boar

Tusks are one of the major factors in judging "trophy" hogs. Older, heavier boars usually have the longest tusks.

up with the tusks. On these animals, the tusks will continue to grow until eventually broken off from rooting or other daily activities.

Love them or hate them, hogs are here to stay—much to the dissatisfaction of many wildlife agencies. Ask for an opinion from any hunter who has enjoyed the thrill of a hog hunt and he will likely recount his tale with a smile and a spark in his eye. Ask a wildlife biologist who has hogs in his assigned territory, and he will likely frown and then invite you to hunt.

My recommendation is to find an area with an abundance of hogs and have fun. Reducing their population is good for the environment, and hogs provide as much excitement as you can find in the hunting world. They're also excellent on the table.

Chapter 2

HUNTING METHODS

There are several good methods for hunting wild hogs. One may be better than the others in a given set of circumstances, so it pays to be adaptable. Critters may alter their habits as a result of hunting pressure or habitat changes, or one method may suit your personal hunting style better than another. Hunters who yearn for raw excitement can chase after a pack of dogs, while those who prefer a more sedate approach can sit and watch a feeding station. And there's always spot-and-stalk or still-hunting for those who really want to test their skills.

HUNTING OVER BAIT

Hunting over bait is usually the most productive way to bring home hogs. While some hunters may scowl at the thought of hunting over bait, it's not always an easy task. Most hogs come in with great caution, just like any other wild critter that has been swatted at a time or two while going to the dinner table. They often come in only under cover of darkness, usually from downwind to check for potential danger, and they flee at the smallest hint of trouble.

More hunters take hogs over bait than by any other method.

After hunting near a bait source, you'll quickly learn that nothing is a sure thing. However, baiting does shift the odds considerably in favor of the hunter.

On one particular occasion, I was hunting near a feeding station when a group of hogs came to eat. The group consisted of hogs of various sizes, and they were extremely nervous. At the snap of a twig they would tense up and bustle about, then stop to survey their surroundings. The hog I was hoping to bag was a large boar that somehow managed to stay in the middle of the pack. Afterwards, I swore that he intentionally used the smaller pigs as shields.

I waited patiently for a clear shot as they mingled about, sucking up corn like vacuum cleaners. I kept the crosshairs fixed squarely behind the shoulder of my target. Just like a sniper lying in wait, the second the shooting lane was clear I

Hunting Methods

was prepared to trip the trigger. The group ate until nearly every bit of corn was gone.

Just as the smaller pigs that surrounded my boar began to break up, which would have allowed an open shot, the familiar whirr of the feeder began. Many times, this sound is what attracts animals to a feeding station, as they become habituated to an easy meal. But you would have thought these hogs had seen the devil himself as they fled from the opening. In a flash, they disappeared into the thick vegetation that bordered the feeding area. The noise they made as they crashed through the brush could be heard for at least a hundred yards or more.

Needless to say, I went home empty-handed that day. The group's movements thwarted my efforts at picking out the best animal, and their nervousness put them on the run before I could sort things out. Not even baiting works every time out.

Feeding stations bring wild hogs back to an area consistently, making hunting in heavy cover much easier.

Preferred baits can vary from dried foods made specifically for attracting hogs to meat from old deer carcasses shot during the fall season. Hogs are happy to consume almost anything. But probably the most popular, cost effective, and readily available food source is whole grain corn. Corn is also a good source of carbohydrates, which will provide the hunter with fatter hogs at the bait station.

Most hunters do a bit of scouting before determining the exact placement of a feeding station. As long as you're in decent hog country, where you place a feeder isn't really that critical; most hogs will find the free food in short order, even if the offerings are in an out-of-the-way location. Still, the best locations for consistent visitation are in areas with one or more well-used hog trails nearby. Start by spreading bait onto the trails using a container or with gloves on to hide your scent. Create a food trail that leads the animals to the feeding area you've set up.

There are several options for keeping bait available. Timed feeders seem to work best, as they can be set to provide only a limited amount of food at predetermined times each day. Any hogs in the area will soon learn that if they aren't at the station on time, they could miss an easy meal.

Another issue to consider is how long a supply of bait will last before it needs to be replenished. If you're loading fifty pounds of corn, the feeder will likely empty out within a couple of weeks. But two hundred pounds or so should last for a couple of months. Using larger amounts does two things for the hunter. It prevents excessive trips into the area and reduces the amount of human scent, both of which lead to less spooky hogs that are more comfortable returning to bait stations again and again.

Moultrie Feeders (1–800–653–3334) is one of the top names in the feeder business. They make feeders in a variety of sizes, but one that quickly caught my attention was the Magnum Fifty-

Hunting Methods

Five-Gallon Tripod Feeder. It holds a whopping four hundred pounds of feed, enough for up to three months.

Other feeding options are also available, but the major drawback to many of these is that they make a much larger portion of food available to wildlife, often the entire amount. If hogs are abundant in the area, they can easily wipe out fifty pounds or more of shelled corn in just a few days. Hogs that feed at stations like this tend to be a bit unpredictable, as they can simply feed at any time, day or night. Timed feeders, although more expensive, require less work and keep hogs coming in regularly at times more advantageous to the hunter.

It's possible for do-it-yourselfers to make their own feeders. These don't work quite as well as timed feeders, but it's possible to build a half-dozen or more for the price of one quality timed feeder.

An excellent compromise is to use both types. Place several cheap feeders in strategic locations throughout the property

It takes a lot of work to maintain bait stations for any length of time, but you'll be well rewarded when you head afield to hunt.

being hunted. All the feeding stations will probably be visited at one time or another, but it should eventually become clear which ones the hogs like best. This can be due to available cover, trails leading to the food source, or a variety of other factors. After you determine which spot the hogs seem to favor most, simply remove all of the homemade feeders and put out your one timed feeder in that location. This will save you money in the long run and still bring hogs in regularly.

PIPE FEEDERS

Pipe feeders are easy to make and can be a great project for the entire family. These feeders work well on hogs, as well as other wildlife. The materials for a pipe feeder include a four- to five-foot section of at least four-inch plastic pipe—PVC works great—an appropriately-sized end cap, an elbow, and some epoxy.

Start by cutting off one foot of pipe. Then join the longer section to the elbow with epoxy. Next, insert the one-foot section of pipe into the other side of the elbow. Finish by sawing off the upper half of the one-foot-long section. The feeder is now ready to use. Find an area with plenty of sign, fill the long section with corn, install the cap, and securely attach the feeder to a tree using bungee cords.

Feeder size can vary with personal preference. The recommendations above may be too small for what you have in mind. Some hunters use six-inch diameter or larger pipe and add a reducer on one end so coupling to a four-inch elbow is easier. It's also possible to use a T-joint, which makes food available in two locations rather than just one. I would recommend sticking with the four-inch outlet, though, so you can limit the rate at which food is dispensed.

You can modify this feeder into a freestanding model simply by attaching the pipe to a two-square-foot section of plywood with

L-brackets (the platform can be made smaller, but doing so may cause instability). Leave just enough room at the junction of the pipe and plywood to allow the bait to slowly trickle out. The possibilities for other variations are endless.

STAND HUNTING

Hunting near a known travel route or natural food source can also lead to success. And this may be the best option for hunters who don't have the free time or resources to deal with all the aspects of baiting. To do a good job with feeding stations, a hunter must not only scout well but also keep bait available consistently enough, and far enough in advance, to condition the hogs in a given area to a specific feeding location and timeframe.

The most attractive natural foods are any hard mast, followed by obvious soft mast or concentrated food sources like

Abandoned home sites are excellent places to search for sign. Many such areas have old fruit orchards and adjacent pastures or meadows.

The Complete Book of Wild Boar Hunting

For the hog hunter, finding a patch of producing oaks is like hitting pay dirt. (California Department of Fish and Game)

gardens or orchards. Hard mast can generally be found throughout good hog habitat, so in years with a good mast crop the wise hunter will waste no time in setting up near an oak full of acorns where hog sign is prevalent. In years where hard mast such as acorns from white oaks, red oaks, and live oaks are scarce, I have found ample hog sign in areas with a lot of hickory nuts, as well as the less favored chestnuts. An area that is very productive one year may be literally worthless the next. Only scouting will clue you in to the best spots under a given set of conditions.

CHOOSING A STAND OR A BLIND

There are many types of stands and blinds on the market these days, and selecting one is really a matter of personal choice. While some are better than others, most will provide satisfactory results. Ideally, a stand should be easy to use, comfortable to sit in

Hunting Methods

for long periods of time, and light enough that portability isn't a problem. For blinds, there are a few slightly different requirements. A blind should be lightweight, easy to construct, and durable enough to withstand the elements.

A portable stand is one of the most popular choices because it allows the hunter to get above the line of sight of any hogs that may be in the area, and depending on the wind currents, a stand can help keep the hunter's scent well above the ground where hogs may pick it up. A stand can also provide the hunter with a bird's-eye view of the surroundings.

Blinds like this one manufactured by Double Bull are great for areas that can't be hunted from a treestand. Hogs usually pay no attention to blinds that blend in well.

Try to find a tree that is larger in diameter than your torso, which will help break up your outline. While this isn't as important for hog hunting as it is for chasing whitetails, in hard-hunted areas a hog will quickly learn to watch more carefully for signs like this. At the first hint, they'll quickly dive for cover.

In areas where suitable trees aren't readily available, or for the hunter who simply prefers to stay at ground level, portable blinds are the ticket. With the recent advances in materials, these

A treestand puts the hunter above a hog's line of sight, improves the field of view in thick cover, and may help reduce scent.

blinds are nothing short of amazing. Most weigh less than twenty pounds and are very easy to put up and take down—some models can be assembled in less than a minute. Camouflage coloring makes them virtually invisible when placed adjacent to existing brush.

For the novice or young hunter, who may have trouble sitting motionless for hours, a portable blind provides a hiding place where the chance of getting caught while moving at the wrong time is nearly eliminated. Double Bull Archery (1–866–614–5545) makes a top-of-the-line blind with all the desired attributes. With the aid of a Double Bull T-5, my son Justin was able to harvest his first animal with a bow—a wild hog, of course.

STALKING AND STILL-HUNTING

If a hunter wants to go one-on-one with a hog, there is no better choice than stalking. Stalking isn't for the timid or those with insufficient knowledge, as it forces the hunter to use all of his senses and woodsmanship while slipping quietly through the hog's

Hunting Methods

home turf. Getting in position for a close-range shot at what can sometimes be an aggressive animal is the ultimate test of skill and nerve.

The stalking hunter can improve his odds in several ways. First, he must know the terrain well and understand wild hog behavior. He must also pay close attention to the wind direction. Never underestimate the scenting ability of a wild hog.

While still-hunting for hogs in southern Alabama I had the opportunity to observe first-hand the sensitivity of a hog's nose. I was slipping along a very thick palmetto patch when I heard the telltale sound of a hog walking along the edge. I had been careful to keep the wind in my face or quartering slightly in my favor. I picked out an opening I thought the tusker would soon pass through and readied for a shot.

Wild hogs know how to use cover to their advantage, which makes still-hunting a real challenge at times. (California Department of Fish and Game)

As the foliage was thick, I had to wait patiently for the hog to walk into the opening far enough to expose its vitals. Eventually, the hog, a light-tan beast with large black spots, poked his head free of the palmetto blades. Just then—like a bad dream—the breeze shifted. The hog gave a flicker of recognition and made a hasty retreat. It sounded like a herd of stampeding cattle was beating its way through the brush.

There was nothing I could do; it was just bad luck. But it was a good reminder that it always pays to respect the hog's sense of smell.

Hogs generally have a fairly small home range, as long as food and cover are readily available. The hunter who understands this can often pinpoint the home range of a pack simply by observing the available sign. Most hogs will remain in their home range unless spooked by excessive human scent or movement. So

This prize is the result of a long morning of spot-and-stalk and still-hunting. (Eric Smith)

Hunting Methods

take extra precaution when entering an area. What follows are some tips to avoid disturbing hogs to the point of abandoning an area while still-hunting.

1. Scent control can't be stressed enough. Always wash with scent-free soap before heading afield, especially from late spring through early fall. Then put on scent-free anti-perspirant and use scent-eliminator sprays like Scent Blocker on your gear and clothing. Also, wear a scent-dampening outfit from one of the major brands. Don't allow any hunting clothing to come in contact with smells that aren't natural to the woods. Wear boots that don't leave scent, preferably an all-rubber design.
2. Avoid stalking through an area more than once every three or four days. This is strictly my own opinion, but I have had much better results after leaving an area for several days, or even a week, before returning to hunt.
3. In areas of thick cover, limit still-hunting to the morning and midday hours. Hogs are naturally more active in the evening hours, so you're more likely to "bump" an animal at this time of day. This isn't as big an issue in more open areas, where spot-and-stalk techniques can be employed. In my experience, evenings are best reserved for hunting from a stand.
4. Avoid entering the core of a known bedding area. Though the goal during midday is to find a bedded hog, accidentally stumbling into a group could push them out of the area for several days.
5. Where possible, use a boat to enter and exit an area. This method of travel is usually much quieter than walking, allowing the hunter to get into prime territory without spooking animals.

CALLING

Hogs seem to be more vocal than a lot of other game animals. The sounds of squeals and grunts are quite common in areas with high populations of wild hogs, and the meaning of these calls can change with tone, urgency, or repetitiveness. It's sometimes possible to call wild hogs in to the gun by duplicating such sounds, although most hunters don't bother with this method because it isn't consistently effective.

The basic grunt is probably the most common hog sound you'll hear in the woods. Its usual function is just to let other members of a group know where an individual is and that everything is okay. This call is normally used during travel and feeding times. In ordinary conditions, it will be monotone and fairly low in volume.

The effectiveness of calling often depends on the terrain being hunted. This area may be better suited to other methods, but it's still good-looking hog habitat.

Hunting Methods

In situations when an animal is scared or being aggressive, this same grunt may be very loud and change in tone depending on the specific hog and the circumstances. Just like a deer's snort, this kind of grunt can be a signal to the group to be on alert for danger. Or it can be a sign of hostility between two animals within a group. Knowing the difference between the two takes experience in the field. You need to observe hogs in a variety of conditions.

You'll pick up the basics quickly, though. Just imagine a child in a small room calling to his mother across the way. To get her attention he will probably talk in a quiet or conversational tone. Now put that same child in a desperate situation, say, lost in the woods. The child may use the same words, but the volume and manner of speaking may differ greatly. It's easy to discern the panicked tone behind the words.

When hunting, I sometimes duplicate this grunt with a commercial deer call. Hogs are very gregarious animals, and they'll often come over to see who is making the noise. Simply sound off every fifteen or twenty minutes, making several low guttural grunts before stopping each session. This should let any hogs within earshot know that another hog is in the area. It may be enough to entice a lonely hog those last few critical yards into shooting range or it may at least draw an unseen hog from dense cover.

The squeal is the second most common sound a hog makes, and it usually means specific danger or pain. A sow being bred, a piglet that becomes separated from a group, or a hog that has just been shot all might squeal. For the hunter, the squeal of a sow being bred is the most important because it means a boar—and more often than not a large boar—is in the area. Noting the location of such a squeal may also help you determine a stand site or still-hunting area for future hunts.

You'll most often hear the squeal of a sow being bred during the last hours of daylight and into the night. It's usually easy to distinguish between the squeal of a piglet and a sow. Most sows I've heard continue squealing for several minutes, while a frightened youngster tends to squeal for only a moment or two before its mother comes running to make sure it is okay. This vocalization can also be used by hunters to attract adult hogs, as they will sometimes rush in to defend what they think is another hog.

Predator calls that simulate a rabbit in distress are effective at times, as they also sound much like a piglet being attacked. It is best to make several excited squeals in a row before stopping to wait for any response. This type of squealing will most often attract sows, but males will often rush in out of curiosity or due to some paternal instinct.

Obviously, the best method for learning how to duplicate the squeals and grunts hogs make is to visit areas with an abundance of hogs and then listen carefully. If that isn't possible, purchase a tape of hog sounds, which you can find on the Internet or by going through magazines that specialize in hog hunting.

HUNTING WITH HOUNDS

Throughout history, hunters have thrilled to the sounds of bellowing hounds chasing game animals. It's now illegal to hunt many species of big game with dogs, but hogs still provide houndsmen with exciting days afield in many regions. It's easy to become addicted to the sport, and once you try it you'll see why.

Many hounds will hunt a variety of animals, while some are trained specifically to find boar, bear, fox, and raccoon. Most serious hunters who utilize hounds agree that it is generally best to concentrate on only one animal. This is especially true in areas where many species share territory.

The most popular breeds for hunting hogs are probably the Plott, redbone, bluetick, and mountain cur. While most of the

Hunting Methods

Most hunters who pursue wild hogs with dogs select larger hounds, although it's really a matter of personal preference.

dogs used for hog hunting are hounds of some kind, they definitely aren't the only pooches that will partake in a hog race. One of the most comical hog hunts I ever experienced was in the company of a pack of dogs that ranged in breed from redbone to mutt.

The mutt, a small beagle mix, was the workhorse of the pack. The little dog had a shrill bark, which sounded like a funny little squeal when he was hot on the trail of a hog. Though small in size, he definitely had the most heart. I believe he actually thought he could whip the 220-pound hog he eventually helped harvest.

The most common method for locating a hog while hunting with hounds is to attach a dog to the hood of a vehicle or in an open dog box. The smartest dog with the best nose is usually placed in this spot, and is often referred to as the "strike dog." The driver then goes slowly along roads and two-tracks that course

Many hunters "hood-rig" a hound with a great nose and then slowly drive country lanes in search of spots where a hog has crossed the road. When the dog strikes scent, all the dogs are released to take up the chase.

through areas known to contain hogs. The eager dog usually pulls hard away from the attachment point on top of the vehicle, trying to reach a few inches farther out in the hope of getting a whiff of hog.

Once the scent reaches a hound's nose, it will literally go crazy, barking and howling incessantly until released to give chase. After the strike dog is set free, the remainder of the pack is released to help. Three

Although it's tough to see in the thick brush, these two hounds have a hog "bayed." He isn't going anywhere.

dogs can usually stop a hog, but without help they may tire, which often makes it easier for the hog to escape once it bays (stands its ground instead of running). This is why a larger pack is advantageous. When the pursuit slows or stops the hunter should move in quickly. If the hog is allowed too much time it could break from the pack and continue running, forcing dogs and hunters to again take up the chase.

DOG TRAINING

Most knowledgeable houndsmen agree that a dog is born with the natural ability and drive to hunt game or it isn't. Although this is certainly true, a burgeoning hog dog still needs some important training to hunt safely and effectively. An entire book could be written about the proper training of hog-hunting dogs, so I won't try to cover every aspect of it here. If you're interested in training a dog for work on hogs the information provided here should point you in the right direction, but I'd urge you to make contact with knowledgeable dog handlers in your area or to join one of the many hound clubs found across the country.

I feel that dog training should begin at a very young age, about seven weeks, and continue through a dog's first birthday. Young dogs are very impressionable and will learn quickly under proper handling. This is also a very important time in forming the bond between master and hunting companion that will last for many years. Most dogs are eager to please their owner, and this desire can be strengthened even more with a good relationship.

Training should begin with basic obedience. The best hog-hunting dog in the world isn't worth much to a hunter if it runs off repeatedly, with no regard for voice commands, or if it won't back off as the hunter prepares for the shot. Basic commands include "sit," "stay," and "come." A dog should be able to perform these commands without hesitation before further training is considered.

After just a few weeks in their new homes, most pups are ready to begin experiencing what their lives will soon revolve around—the smell of a hog. Save some scraps of hog hide or acquire hog parts from other hunters. Begin with a small piece of skin or a section of lower leg, something the pup can handle well. Rub the skin or leg playfully in the pup's face so he can grab it. In most cases, a tug-of-war will ensue. With a little work, you'll be able to throw the hog part a short distance, and the pup will go after the prize and return on command.

As training progresses, conceal a strip of hog hide and allow the pup to search for it. Once the dog masters this game, drag the item through various types of cover, letting the pup search for and find the source of the smell. Start with short trails over ground that is flat and easy to traverse. Don't make these early searches too difficult. A pup has a fairly short attention span, so

Because hogs are tenacious creatures, hounds are sometimes beneficial for following up on wounded animals.

hold off on the longer trails until after he's about six months old. When he's finding the skin with regularity, increase the distance and difficulty of the scent trail.

The best way to finish the training process is to allow the hound to run with a pack, which greatly increases the learning curve. It's unbelievable how quickly a hound will learn exactly what his job is after only a handful of outings. This is especially true if the outings are productive.

This is also make-or-break time, because this is the stage where you learn whether or not the dog has what it takes to be a good hog-hunting dog. If the drive and ability shine through, it may just take a bit more fine tuning. If not, you might have more of a pet than a hunting dog. In most cases, if the breeding is there and the dog has been nurtured, cared for, and diligently trained, you'll end up with a quality dog.

For most hunters, the relationship that grows between dog and hunter becomes more enjoyable than the actual hunting. There is a special bond between a houndsman and his pack. This love and devotion occasionally manifests itself in a dog putting himself in danger to protect his master—truly a sight to behold. On the other side of the relationship is a master that will spare no expense to keep his canine partner happy and healthy.

Hunters who treat their animals with the utmost respect are paid back with a devotion and desire to please that few others will ever know.

Chapter 3

FINDING AND INTERPRETING SIGN

The best hunters are usually skilled woodsmen. A top-notch marksman is out of luck if he can't find anything to shoot. These woodsman skills can only be polished in nature's classroom, the fields and forests. But the information here will put the novice hunter well ahead of the beginner who learns randomly on his own. This chapter is one of the most important in the book because if game can't be found and habits understood the rest won't matter—unless, of course, you happen to run over a hog on your way to work.

To have success hunting any game animal, the hunter must first be able to competently interpret the signs the animal leaves behind while going about its daily routine. Hog hunting is no exception. If a hunter will put in his time learning as much as possible about hog preferences, the type of sign they leave, and the topography of the area being hunted, his odds for success will increase significantly.

The abundance of sign in an area is directly related to the local population of hogs, but in areas where hogs aren't literally everywhere some of the clues can be very subtle. When hogs are known to inhabit an area but sign isn't highly evident, take it slow. These smaller herds, which often see minimal hunting pressure, actually can be more predictable than hogs inhabiting areas with obvious three-inch-deep trails and numerous wallows but with high hunting pressure.

WHERE TO LOOK

Hogs seem to prefer low-lying areas when they're available. These include swamps, swamp edges, bogs, natural springs, and, in both the East and West, areas along creek drainages. Using a topographic map of an area, a hunter should be able to quickly identify areas like these that merit further scouting.

Hogs are also famous for spending a majority of the daylight hours in areas so thick that human travel is nearly impossible. The make-up of this habitat can vary from region to region, but the vegetation is almost always dense. Most hogs in the Southeast tend to concentrate in areas with thick undergrowth and palmettos, while in the West favored hiding places include plum thickets and oak brush. In mountainous terrain, hogs seem to gravitate to laurel and ivy thickets, old clear-cut areas, and, on occasion, rocky bluffs.

Wet, low-lying terrain makes wonderful hog habitat.

Wherever hogs are left alone they are most content.

A primary factor that establishes where a hog spends the majority of his time, no matter the terrain or area being hunted, is the availability of preferred foods. These food sources can be mast from hardwood groves, old or existing fruit orchards, open fields, and gardens, as well as baited areas. In coastal regions, low tide may even bring hogs onto barren shores in search of clams or crustaceans. No matter what hunting method you choose, you can never go wrong by hunting close to a food source.

AGING SIGN

Because hog habitat is very different from region to region—the ground can be muddy, sandy, or very firm—it is sometimes difficult to read sign or determine its age. Becoming adept at deciphering and aging sign is the product of experience, usually within a specific area you come to know well. Some things to consider are how well the sun reaches the forest floor, how much rain occurs in a particular season, wind conditions, and the texture of the soil.

All of these factors may combine to create sign that appears to be much older, or fresher, than is actually the case. Through trial and error, the hunter will learn the effects that the local environment has on sign. For example, how quickly scat deteriorates in the humid, overgrown forests of the Southeast will differ significantly from how it changes over time in the drier, more open country in California. And in some scenarios, due to environmental conditions, sign may never be accurately aged.

TRACKS AND TRAILS

The first obvious signs you'll likely come across while scouting hog country are tracks and trails. Many first-time hog hunters have trouble distinguishing between deer and hog tracks. This is understandable, as both have split hooves that are similar in size. But there are some slight differences that will help you figure it out.

The track of a deer is narrower and more pointed toward the front, whereas a hog track has a blockier appearance. The track of a wild hog actually reminds me more of a pronghorn track, as it's squarer in the front and more uniform in overall width.

One other clue is the presence of many tracks in various sizes near each other, which means that young boars, sows, and juveniles are probably traveling as a group.

In areas with healthy hog populations, trails are usually easy to spot. Hogs seem to be more habitual than deer in traveling one specific path on a regular basis. This holds true unless the hogs are actively feeding, in which case they tend to wander widely, sucking up whatever morsel of nutrition they can find.

Some trails in hog country are worn deeply into the soil, as many generations of hogs have utilized the same travel routes over the years. Fainter trails may be made by older boars that tend to travel alone, or they may simply be the result of a firmer, more rigid soil base. Always consider the terrain when making assessments about trail use.

Hunting along a well-worn trail may be productive at times,

Most hog trails run between bedding and feeding areas, although they may traverse a variety of terrain.

Finding and Interpreting Sign

but because large groups commonly use these routes, a trail may appear to be more heavily traveled than it actually is. If the trail happens to lead to a preferred food source, then placing a stand in the area definitely holds merit. Otherwise, it's best to keep following the trail as it courses through the forest, looking for other sign that will give you a better feel for how hogs are using the area. Most trails will eventually lead to a bedding area, wallow, or feeding area. Use the combination of signs to figure out the best ambush spots.

Be very careful when scouting trails, and leave as little human scent as possible. (Scent-proof your body and clothing, wear rubber-soled boots, and try to avoid contact with surrounding vegetation.) Crashing through the woods and leaving your scent everywhere will put all the hogs in the area on alert, and it may even cause them to leave temporarily.

SCAT

After trails and tracks, hog scat, or droppings, will probably be the most noticeable sign in a hog's home range. At times, groups will designate a specific area just for this activity. The ground in such an area will have an abundance of hog waste. Just like with other game animals, droppings are typically more evident near bedding and feeding areas, as that is where hogs spend most of their time.

With normal diets of roots, tubers, and other vegetation, hog droppings will appear similar in size and texture to that of a young calf. Of course, this depends entirely on an animal's diet.

The consistency of hog scat varies according to available food sources.

Check scat carefully for evidence of what the hog has been feeding on, as this may lead you to local food sources that will help you identify nearby areas of high use.

ROOTING

Hog habitat just wouldn't be complete without an area that has been rooted through by resident hogs. (This activity is one of the main reasons many wildlife biologists would like to see hogs eradicated.) Rooting occurs as hogs use their tusks and snouts to turn up soil. This activity can be scattered or concentrated depending on the season and other available foods.

The most common reason for a hog to turn soil is the search for the delicate roots that exist just under the surface. Rooting activity seems to peak from late spring through fall. Because hogs

While signs of rooting can be found throughout forested country, it is primarily done in green areas that contain young roots and tubers.

Finding and Interpreting Sign

have only one stomach, it is more difficult for them to digest dry, tough grasses. Tender roots and other morsels found underground are much more palatable for them. Grubs and worms also may be found, and these are very rich in nutrients.

At various times of year, hogs may also frequent livestock pastures. If you spot cow patties inadvertently flipped over, it is usually the work of a turkey or hog. If it's a hog, other sign such as tracks or droppings will often be present. The reasons for this scavenging are similar to why they root; underneath those old nasty cow pies are tender grass shoots and the occasional bug.

WALLOWS

Wallows are almost like the community bathhouse for wild hogs. And there's no mistaking a wallow in the woods. Many times, you will smell it before you see it.

These wallows are used with some regularity throughout the warmer months, as they help to reduce the number of insects that continually swarm around and attach themselves to a hog's body. To a hog, a good wallowing session is kind of like what a bath and a shot of bug spray would be to us.

Nearly all wallows are located in moist low-lying

Even muddy roads can serve as wallows.

Wild hogs use mud to stay cool and as protection against biting insects.

areas, but if a muddy area isn't available hogs will simply roll in the dust. The results are evidently similar, but not quite as good. Some areas seem to be more attractive than others as wallow sites. Soil type appears to be a determining factor. Hogs prefer muddy areas with clay-like or very rich soil. This type of soil sticks to their skin and hair much better than looser, sandy soils.

Once you locate a wallow, spend some time studying it. In some situations, the size of a hog can be determined by the marks it leaves in the mud. And the mud around a typical wallow is a great place to find tracks and gauge size.

RUBS

When you locate a wallow, always look for a nearby rub—or vice versa—as they generally go hand in hand. Large, thick-sapped

Finding and Interpreting Sign

Certain trees seem to be preferred as scratching posts or for marking.

trees seem to be the preferred rubbing posts. Of course, this doesn't mean that hogs won't rub other trees. I've heard about hogs rubbing on fence posts, light poles, and the corners of remote buildings or sheds. On one occasion, I even heard of a hog rub on the bumper of an abandoned car. These types of rubs are a rarity, but they do occur.

The reasons for rubbing vary, but when hogs seek out sap-rich trees like pines it's usually to coat their bodies with sap, which helps repel insects. And they also can be looked upon as sign posts and scratching posts.

When you find a rub, check it over carefully. As a boar rubs his head back and forth, his sharp tusks will often scar the tree, revealing clues to his size.

BEDDING AREAS

Bedding areas are most often located under and/or within extremely thick cover. Good examples are old clear-cuts, dense briar thickets, palmetto patches, and beneath fallen trees. Basically, any area that looks like good cover for a rabbit is ideal for a hog.

Be very careful when hunting anywhere even close to a bedding area. As most hogs will already be in the security of their lairs by early morning, any intrusion could cause them to abandon that core area temporarily. And if you repeatedly push hogs from these areas, they may leave permanently.

Whenever possible, I prefer to scout an area at least several days, if not weeks, in advance of my actual hunting dates. If I spot

Bedding grounds are typically located in thick cover. Be sure to search the surrounding area for other sign.

any extremely thick areas during my search, I note them but give them a wide berth. Even when you find hogs in their bedding areas, clear shooting lanes are few and far between. From a hunting perspective, it's much more important to find likely feeding areas, as these are normally located in less dense cover that is easier to hunt.

PUTTING IT ALL TOGETHER

Every bit of sign you find in the field is a valuable tool in determining travel patterns, feeding areas, and the daily routine of hogs in your area. Scouting is very similar to putting together a puzzle. Every piece is essential for a successful outcome.

The wise hunter will put in scouting time, gather information, and then make knowledgeable decisions that place him in the path of his prize.

Chapter
4

Equipment

The right equipment for pursuing hogs, or any game animal, for that matter, can mean the difference between bringing home the bacon or coming home empty-handed. It can also mean the difference between a comfortable hunt and one where bugs are driving you so crazy you miss your chance at a prize hog. In an extreme example, poor equipment could even leave you snakebitten.

Choosing the right weapon for hogs doesn't need to be too complicated. The novice hunter can just use a rifle or bow that is well suited for deer-sized game. The average whitetail weighs approximately 150 pounds, which is about the same as the average hog in most areas, so using similar equipment makes sense. A few exceptions will become evident as you gain experience, but this is a good general starting point.

Hogs are dense, well-built critters compared to most ungulates, and they can take a lot of punishment. This seems to be especially true of any hog that weighs over two hundred pounds. When a boar exceeds this weight it develops thick, gristly side shields that provide a defense against the sharp tusks of other

Wild hogs have thick skins and compact, muscular bodies; shot placement is critical in a quick, clean kill. (Charlie Tanner)

large boars during fights over breeding rights. Ask any taxidermist who mounts his share of hogs and he will likely tell you stories of dulling several knife blades while thinning the shoulder skin of a large boar. It's tough stuff.

SUGGESTED RIFLE CALIBERS

To properly handle these tough animals, gun hunters frequently tote large magnums. Favorites among avid hog hunters include the .30–06, 7mm Remington magnum, and the .300 Winchester magnum. Popular cartridges for short-range hunting—the norm for hog hunting in the South—include the .35 Remington, .45–70 Government, and the new .450 Marlin.

BULLET DESIGN IS CRITICAL

Any seasoned hunter knows that bullet design is critical when hunting tough, dense game. A bullet that breaks up easily will not penetrate properly, while a nonexpanding bullet will zip right through without causing much damage or leaving a suitable blood trail.

Choose a durable bullet design with a slow, controlled expansion rate. This will ensure proper penetration and energy release. Prime examples designed for centerfire rifles include the Trophy Bonded Bear Claw, Swift A-Frame, Winchester's Fail-Safe, and the Barnes X-Bullet.

Equipment

Lever-action rifles are the choice of many hog hunters, but semi-autos are also popular. (Steve Smith)

OTHER FIREARMS

Muzzleloaders with appropriate loads are also quite effective for hogs, particularly as most shots come at fairly short distances. Modern propellants, magnum loads, and well-constructed bullets make these weapons a good choice. Most muzzleloading hog hunters prefer a .54 caliber, and a .50 caliber should be considered the minimum.

Shotguns are also used extensively in the South, where short distances are the norm and quick follow-up shots may be necessary. Shotgun users should go no lighter than 12-gauge, and may even want to drop down to 10-gauge. Either gauge is capable of putting down the largest of hogs.

Proper loads for the shotgun are largely influenced by personal preference and local tradition. Buckshot and slugs will both

The Complete Book of Wild Boar Hunting

Handguns are a good choice for many close-range shooting situations. (Howard Communications)

do the job, but because hogs tend not to bleed profusely slugs are often the better option. They inflict more shock and create a larger wound channel.

Most shotgun hunters choose autoloaders or pump guns. These actions are well built and offer very fast reloading, something you may appreciate when a wounded hog barrels past you.

Because hog hunting is generally a close-range activity, many hunters opt for a handgun. They are particularly useful for hunters following dogs or sitting over bait piles because shots in these situations usually take place at distances under forty yards, often much closer. And if you're chasing hounds all day through thick brush, a holstered handgun is much easier to tote around than a heavy rifle. Because the action can be fast at times, scopes aren't really necessary for handguns.

Equipment

Most hunters stick with the larger calibers available when handgun hunting for hogs. Some hunters who load their own ammo may go as small as the .357 magnum, but the .44 magnum is probably the most popular caliber. Other favored calibers include the .41 magnum, .45 Long Colt, and the .454 Cassull. Revolvers are easily the most preferred action, but some large semi-autos and single actions are also used.

ARCHERY EQUIPMENT

Bowhunting is also a viable choice for hog hunting, and it presents an enjoyable challenge. But because archery equipment doesn't kill with raw energy, the bowhunter's equipment should be suitable for sending an arrow through thick skin, muscle, and fat. For smaller hogs, the bow and arrows you use on deer will

Most archers that hunt hogs stick with modern compound bows.

usually do the trick (40 pounds or more), but for hogs nearing the 200-pound mark, a 60-pound draw weight should be considered the minimum, with 70 pounds or more even better.

The compound is the most widely used type of bow. But the recurve and the longbow can also be effective under the right circumstances. Because kinetic energy is slightly lower from a traditional bow than a compound, weight minimums should be bumped up a bit. These minimums will vary based on arrow choice and broadhead design. A heavier arrow absorbs more of the bow's energy than a lighter arrow, and cut-on-contact broadheads tend to need less energy for penetration than a chisel point. An open-on-contact (mechanical) broadhead requires the most. To keep things simple, just consider fifty pounds the minimum for traditional equipment.

Archery equipment has changed dramatically since I first started using it in the 1970s, and this includes arrow shafts. Today the bowhunter can choose between wood, aluminum, and carbon. Wood is really only used with traditional equipment these days; aluminum is probably the most popular shaft available; and carbon, while still fairly new, rivals aluminum in durability and has excellent penetration qualities because of its small diameter. Carbon shafts also don't bend or break as often as the others. Any of these materials will serve the archer well, but a good general rule for hog hunters is to choose a shaft on the heavy side. Thick-walled aluminum shafts and most carbon shafts are excellent options.

One of the most important factors when choosing archery gear is the business end of the arrow—the broadhead. Opinions about which broadhead is best vary widely based on personal preference. My favorite is a four-blade, 115-grain Muzzy. It's one of the most durable designs on the market. The Muzzy broadhead is virtually indestructible, which is very important when

Equipment

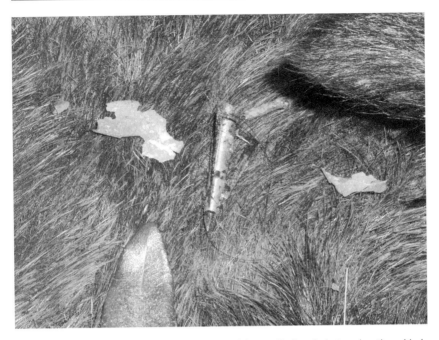

A hunting partner took this large boar down with a well-placed shot and a three-blade Muzzy broadhead. (Eric Smith)

you're trying to put an arrow through the tough hide and body of a big hog.

The largest hog I've taken tipped the scales just shy of 250 pounds, and my Mathews Q2XL, at 72 pounds of draw weight, sent the Muzzy tip zipping through his ribs like hot butter. Other durable heads include Thunderhead, Rocky Mountain, or Wasp in 100- or 125-grain models.

Some archers prefer a cut-on-contact broadhead like the Zwickey or the Snuffer, and these work great if properly sharpened. I'd recommend avoiding mechanical broadheads for hog hunting, though. Mechanical heads work great on thin-skinned animals such as deer or antelope, but they may not function properly on a large, tough boar.

SHOT PLACEMENT

Although weapons with plenty of punch are advantageous for taking hogs down quickly and cleanly, nothing is more important than shot placement. Almost any modern firearm can kill a hog if the situation is ideal—meaning a perfectly placed shot behind the shoulder on a perfectly positioned hog. It's when hunters take shots when things aren't perfect, which seems to be most of the time, that the extra firepower is needed.

Hogs also differ a bit anatomically from deer. Hunters are usually taught to shoot behind the shoulder of deer-sized game, and this rule is absolutely mandatory for hogs. Their thick skin, coupled with stout shoulder blades, are impenetrable for all but the most powerful firearms.

When injured, a hog may use its formidable tusks to attack a hunter, his dogs, or whatever else gets in the way. (Eric Smith)

Equipment

Also, while field dressing and butchering, you will notice that the vital organs sit in the lower two-thirds of the chest cavity, so keep any shots a bit lower than usual for short tracking jobs.

Shot placement is particularly critical for archers. Because all hogs are laden with fat, an arrow hole can be plugged quickly, allowing little, if any, blood to escape. And in swampy or very thick areas, which are common in most hog habitat in the Southeast, a marginally hit hog that ventures several hundred yards before expiring may never be found. There just won't be much of a blood trail to follow.

To take hogs with any consistency, a bowhunter must practice regularly well in advance of any hunting trip. (Eric Smith)

And if you hit the shoulder blade, you might as well forget that hog. I hate to admit it, but during one hunt I had a chance at a beautiful, jet-black boar that probably weighed in at 150 pounds. His tusks protruded at least an inch and a half, and he was a real keeper. When the shot opportunity presented itself I attempted to tuck the arrow right behind the shoulder. But rather than threading the needle perfectly, I hit the hog squarely in the shoulder.

I found all but the forward-most inch of my arrow. The hog may have been sore for a while, but he certainly lived to fight another day.

The ideal shot is broadside or quartering slightly away, which should allow the projectile to pierce both lungs. Think carefully before pulling the trigger or letting that arrow go at any other shot angles. No hunter should risk leaving a wounded animal in the field, and following up on a wounded boar can be dangerous, particularly in thick cover.

SPECIALTY ITEMS

In this modern age of hunting, there seems to be a specialty item for almost any conceivable need. Scent eliminators, attractants, Gore-Tex clothing, GPS units — the list is endless. Some of these items aren't really necessary, but many will help you find more success in the field.

Equipment that protects you from the elements or biting insects allows you to hunt longer and more comfortably. In very warm weather, this might include snakeproof boots or chaps, breathable clothing, and bug spray, while insulated boots and quality cold-weather clothing is in order for snowy, frigid days.

A game cart can save a lot of wear and tear on your back and the animal's hide.

Ordinary hunting clothes will suffice for many hunts, but having these specialty items can make outings much more comfortable and safe, allowing you to concentrate fully on the task at hand.

CLOTHING AND FOOTWEAR

Appropriate clothing and boots are essential for an enjoyable hunt, and circumstances will dictate the right choices. Hunters who traipse after a dog pack in the mountains of Tennessee may just wear jeans and a T-shirt, a light jacket, and a pair of comfortable hiking boots. But most hog hunts differ significantly. You may have to hike through the cactus- and thorn-covered deserts of Texas and Arizona or still-hunt along the edges of a swamp on a humid day in Georgia or sit on stand in New Hampshire in December.

Just remember, comfort is a major key to success in the field. I'll go into more detail on specialized gear for summer outings in the next chapter, but the following regional rundown should give you an idea about what will work best in any given set of conditions.

THE SOUTHEAST

Many hunters think of the Southeast as flat and swampy, but the truth is that this region includes many different types of terrain. From the rolling hardwood hills to the many cotton and soybean fields, hogs have a lot of habitat choices. Still, I would have to concede that a majority of the hog hunting in the Southeast does take place adjacent to, or right in the middle of, a swamp.

For hunters of the lowlands, waterproof footwear is essential. An excellent starting point is a pair of rubber boots that are sixteen inches or more in height. Most modern all-rubber boots fit well, and some even have adjustable straps for the calf area and form-fitting foot areas. Some hunters opt for waders, but I wouldn't

The Complete Book of Wild Boar Hunting

A good pair of boots and loose, comfortable clothing will make your hunt more enjoyable.

recommend venturing into an area where waders are necessary; that is what boats are for.

The Southeast isn't known for extremely cold temperatures, although a Florida hunter who spends all day sitting on stand during a January cold snap might beg to differ. When the temperature drops, choose a pair of all-rubber boots with 400 grams or more of insulation and wear socks with a high wool content. Also, wear perspiration-wicking liners next to the skin. Feet tend to sweat more in all-rubber boots, and these liners will help keep them dry, an essential element in keeping warm.

Light, loose-fitting clothing is usually the norm in the warmer months. In colder weather, add insulated bib overalls and a coat. Bibs are a good choice because they double insulate the chest area when worn with a coat overtop. On warmer days, above 40 degrees or so, they can be worn comfortably without a coat.

THE SOUTHWEST

Javelina and an abundance of wild hogs call the southwestern deserts and Texas mesquite flats home. Certain attributes are a given for this area: It's arid, full of cactus or thorny vegetation, and temperatures can vary more than 40 degrees in a day. This is a harsh environment, but if you take the proper precautions your hunting trip here will be nothing short of fantastic.

As with other areas, footwear is a major factor for comfort. Many plants in the Southwest have stickers or thorns, so it's all too easy to be put out of commission by an injured foot. To pursue critters here, it's often necessary to walk great distances, which means protecting your feet is job one. Boots should be very rugged and durable. I would recommend a well-built, all-leather design with a height of at least ten inches. Heavy Cordura will work in a pinch, but it doesn't turn away thorns like leather.

With the drastic temperature changes that are possible here, layering your clothing is the best approach. At dawn, the temperature could be in the teens, but by midafternoon it may climb to sixty or more. Wear a pair of moisture-wicking, medium to light, full-body underwear under loose clothing, and top this off with a medium to heavy jacket. It's wise to wear a heavy coat and pack along a light jacket for warmer hours of the day.

THE NORTHEAST

In most hunting seasons, consecutive days with 30-degree temperatures are considered normal in the Northeast, so warmth becomes the primary issue. Hunters who sit on stand should take particular care in choosing clothing, as they don't have the option of moving around to increase circulation.

Extremely cold weather calls for footwear of a pack-boot design. These boots are the only thing I've found that will keep my feet warm in the coldest temperatures. Find a pair with at least 800 grams of Thinsulate. Some designs can be very bulky, as they provide an incredible amount of insulation.

Moisture is the primary culprit in cold feet. Your feet may not feel wet, but your feet will sweat enough to dampen your socks even when simply walking. For this reason, it is advisable to change socks once you reach the stand. Also, sock material is very important. Read the labels that come with all socks. Most socks that come in bulk will be primarily polyester, cotton, or some other undesirable material. Always choose a sock manufactured with at least 70-percent wool. Though some grades of wool are warmer than others, any type will be warmer than most other materials.

If this isn't enough, take along a pair of boot blankets and foot warmers. Be careful not to use hand warmers for this application, though, as the two differ in the amount of oxygen they need to work and the temperatures they reach.

Layering is key for the rest of your outfit. Begin with heavyweight, insulated long underwear. Wear lofty pants and a shirt over this. Wool is preferable, but can be expensive. Another excellent material for the second layer is a fleece suit. Top this off with insulated bibs and a parka that extends below the waist.

Because a person is only as warm as his head and hands, wear a full facemask and a pair of Glo-mitts. The latter are gloves with the fingers removed at the first joint and removable mittens sewn to the backs. These are easy to remove when an animal comes into view, but protect bare skin the rest of the time.

QUALITY OPTICS

It is amazing how many sportsmen go to the ends of the earth to pursue game, yet settle for cheap equipment. This makes no sense to me. You'll always appreciate quality optics, and they'll last a long, long time.

After doing research, putting in for a tag, traveling, and arranging for food and lodging, the last thing you want is a problem that could easily have been avoided. For some reason, optics tend to fall low on the list of important items, when in reality they should be near the top. You can't shoot what you can't see.

I highly recommend Nikon products. That is not to say that other quality optics don't exist—they certainly do—but I've had great success with this brand.

Equipment

Using a quality laser rangefinder to identify exact distances can mean the difference between success and failure.

Whatever brand you choose, make certain it's waterproof to the point of submersion. Some claim to be water-resistant, which simply means they will repel water in a light rain shower. But for most hunters, Murphy's Law usually rings true at the worst times—at least it does for me.

BINOCULARS

Binoculars should be close at hand no matter what the hunting situation. They can be used for anything from glassing a distant hillside to deciphering movement in thick brush to picking out animals in low light.

For hunting in the Southeast, where cover is very thick, I recommend magnifications of 7×35 or 8×40. Those who are weight conscious may opt for a pair of compact 8×21 binocs. When choosing between large or compact binoculars, remember that the exit pupil is much larger in the full-sized model, which allows much more light to reach the eye. This translates to better vision in low-light conditions.

To determine the exit pupil of a binocular (measured in millimeters), divide the objective lens diameter by the power of the binocular. So for 7 × 21, the result would be three millimeters. In 8 × 40, it's five millimeters, which is almost twice as large. As the human eye can only handle somewhere around five millimeters, there probably isn't much sense in going larger than this. But it also makes sense to maximize the benefits as much as possible.

In open country, a pair of full-sized binoculars may be the most important tool a hunter carries after his weapon. In situa-

Binoculars are essential in all types of terrain. Never leave home without them.

tions where you need to do a lot of glassing, as is the case with javelina hunting or hunting California hogs, choose a top brand with magnification of 10 × 40 or 12 × 50. A pair that sits comfortably in the hands is advisable, as you may be holding them for many hours over the course of a season.

Again, even when picking a full-sized binocular, remember the exit-pupil formula. If both are of equal quality, opt for 10 × 50 over 10 × 40.

RIFLE SCOPES

Though many hunters use open sights for close-range work, the majority top their firearms with scopes. A scope offers a clearer, magnified sight picture. For shots of less than a hundred yards, a fixed-power, 4X-scope is ideal.

Fixed-power scopes are very durable, and they're usually much cheaper than variables from the same manufacturer. Also, the exit pupil on a fixed, low-power scope is usually great. You can achieve the same results with a variable scope by turning it to a lower power. Variable scopes make sense if you hunt a variety of game animals from a variety of distances with the same rifle, but most hunters shoot with more consistent accuracy if they stick to one magnification they're comfortable with.

SPOTTING SCOPES

If you primarily hunt in the swamps of the Southeast, a spotting scope is next to useless. On the other hand, if you hunt the open country of the Southwest and California, it can be invaluable.

A spotting scope is great for determining the size of individual animals, and it can also help you determine the best stalking route. Small ditches and other breaks in the terrain that might otherwise go unnoticed can be readily seen with most spotting scopes.

Choose one that will increase to almost 40X. An objective lens of at least sixty millimeters provides excellent clarity at such large magnification.

DON'T GET LOST

The best hog-hunting country is often swampy, flat, dense, and otherwise featureless. And unless you have an intimate knowledge of the property being hunted, it's easy to become disoriented after traveling only several hundred yards from a road or trail.

In recent years, Global Positioning Systems (GPS) have made waves in the hunting community. Many sportsmen now carry these handy little gadgets. GPS units were difficult to use and of suspect accuracy when first introduced, but today's models are affordable and boast unbelievable accuracy. Most high-end units will even work well under a canopy of thick foliage.

Compasses still have their place, of course, and most knowledgeable navigators recommend carrying both while in the field. As the GPS unit is electronic, malfunctions are always a possibility. Use your compass to verify the GPS reading. If they agree, you're in the clear. If not, trust the compass, unless it has been severely damaged.

Chapter 5

Year-Round Hunting

A major appeal for hog hunters is that when all other seasons are closed in many states, hog season remains open. Also, hog hunting isn't confined to certain dates in many areas, so hogs can sometimes be hunted in combination with other game.

Though the hottest months of the year—July and August—typically see a reduction in the number of hunters pursuing tuskers, the option is still available for anyone who can't resist the challenge of a summer hunt. Just remember that you may need to modify your hunting tactics, equipment, and game-care practices.

Heat, bugs, and snakes are common at this time of year, especially in the Southeast, which is considered a prime destination for year-round hunting. But by following a few simple rules your summer hog outing can be much more enjoyable, if not downright comfortable.

SNAKES

Probably the most worrisome aspect of summer hunting for most folks is the prospect of a snake encounter. Despite the fact that very few individuals are bitten each year, there is something about snakes that keeps many hunters out of the woods. You're actually far more likely to be bothered by biting insects and the heat when hunting in warm weather. Still, pushing snakes out of your thoughts isn't easy.

On a recent mid-August hunt in the swamps of South Carolina, the guide told me that the chance of seeing a water moccasin (cottonmouth) was pretty high. This statement made me a bit queasy, particularly because he said it just as we passed under some low-hanging branches along the water's edge on the way to my stand.

That first morning I continually looked above, below, and to the side of my stand for any snakes. Near ten o'clock, I heard the faint sound of my guide returning for me. My nerves had settled a bit by then, at least until I happened to look beneath me. I have no clue where it came from, but a long—at least four feet—dark snake was swimming along the surface of the water, within feet of the tree where I was positioned.

Seeing one of these guys may make you forget all about snakes. Alligators, snakes, and wild hogs share habitat in many areas of the

I quickly studied the head, which was at least three inches across—definitely a viper. The hair on the back of my neck stood on end as I watched the reptile glide past the base of my perch. As the sound of the guide's boat neared, the snake quickly crawled out of the water and slid into a thick brush pile. Cautiously, I climbed down and crawled aboard the only reasonable means of transportation out of the swamp.

I never encountered another reptile during the remainder of that trip; but that is not to say the scaly critters weren't on my mind.

SNAKES AREN'T OUT TO GET YOU

Believe it or not, snakes are equally, if not more, scared of us than we are of them. In the encounter above, as soon as the snake was aware of a human presence it tried to avoid a confrontation. If a snake can get into a hiding place, it will usually be long gone before you ever have a chance to see it.

A snake's venom is used for two purposes: it helps the snake acquire food and, on rare occasions, provides a means of self-defense. Using venom for self-defense is usually a snake's last resort because it can take several days to replenish the lost venom, which can mean no food for a while.

The only time a snake will strike a large mammal is if it feels threatened. A snake isn't a vile, aggressive creature; rather, it simply doesn't know what kind of danger you represent. It just reacts to a given situation.

TIPS FOR AVOIDING SNAKES

Even equipped with this knowledge, it's a good idea to know how to avoid encounters with snakes. Start by trying to stay out of areas known to harbor snakes. This can often be difficult in hog country, but when given the choice, walk on dry open ground.

Also, pay close attention to low-hanging branches. Snakes will often stretch out along thick branches while sunning. They usually abandon their perch, dropping to the ground or into the water, long before a hunter arrives, but if you are gliding along quietly in search of a hog the snake may not hear you coming.

Be particularly cautious when entering a boat, treestand, blind, or any outdoor vehicle or structure that may offer a suitable hiding place for snakes.

PROTECTION

Even while trying to avoid snakes, it's best to prepare for the worst—an attempted bite. Wear snake-proof clothing below the knee and quality boots. Many people think that a snake strikes with enough power to penetrate almost any material or that a bite can knock the victim off his feet. This couldn't be further from the truth.

A small percentage of snakebite victims don't even know they've been bitten until they feel a burning sensation in the bite area. And misses occur fairly often. Even when the snake hits its mark, loose jeans or hunting pants can stop penetration into the leg.

If you are actually bitten, it may not be of immediate comfort to know that because snakes are expending and replenishing venom on a regular basis, there is a good chance that not much venom will be transferred into the bite. But you'll be happy later.

Snake-proof boots are widely available these days, and I highly recommend them to hog hunters who'll be out in the warmer months. Several brands are also waterproof and quite tall, extending almost to the knee. These will serve you well in swampy conditions. If you don't want to lay out the extra bucks for snake boots, there's a cheaper option. Snake protectors can be worn over your boots and pants, and most sell for fifty dollars or less.

Statistics show that most snakebites are below the knee, with bites on the hand a distant second, so a snake boot should be all the protection you need in most cases. As for protecting your hands, just be careful when lifting a log or reaching into a crevice. Use a stick to probe around first.

If the area you plan to hunt is primarily swamp or marsh, you may want to opt for a pair of knee-high rubber boots. All rubber boots are strong enough to fend off the strike of any snake—or so I've been told. Luckily, I've never had to test this theory during a hog outing.

A pair of snake-proof boots or rubber boots that cover the calf will fend off nearly all strike attempts by snakes, although such situations are rare.

If you want real peace of mind, spend the extra dough to acquire high-quality snake-proof boots.

BUGS

Biting insects are more irritating than life threatening, although many diseases can be transmitted from bugs like mosquitoes. Bugs can drive a hunter to the brink of insanity, as most early-season deer hunters can attest. It's virtually impossible to have an enjoyable time with a swarm of mosquitoes and gnats around your head, but proper preparation can virtually eliminate this problem.

And with the spread of diseases like West Nile virus (mosquitoes) and Lyme disease (ticks), it's just good sense to protect yourself.

All kinds of bug sprays are available, and most will work fine; however, all but a few are smelly and some can irritate sensitive skin. Bug suits have become increasingly popular in recent years. These are designed to enclose the entire body and prohibit insects from reaching the skin's surface.

One of the best I've used is produced by Bug-Out Outdoorwear, Inc. It's made of an ultra-fine mesh that joins well at the gloves, head net, and midsection. The suit I chose even in-

Don't forget to pack that bug suit along with your other gear when hunting in warm weather.

cludes a scent-eliminating system to boost scent control, a major plus when hunting during the summer. The suit was extremely light and breathable compared to other scent-eliminating systems, which helps alleviate heat problems. During a hot-weather hog trip to Florida recently, my bug suit worked flawlessly. Swarms of mosquitoes hovered nearby but couldn't get to me.

One recent innovation that works very well is a mosquito repellant by ThermaCell (www.mosquitorepellant.com). This device uses propane to heat a bug-deterring wafer that releases bug repellant. No suits or bug dope are required. In situations with very little or no wind, the fumes prevent most insects from getting anywhere near you. And when the wind picks up, bugs usually present fewer problems anyway.

SUMMER HUNTING CLOTHING

In my opinion, it is much easier to dress for cold temperatures than for hot. But several options exist that will help you avoid overheating. First, choose a material that helps wick moisture away from the body. The most common T-shirt material is cotton, which is certainly comfortable, yet it is one of the worst materials you can wear because it readily holds moisture. Excess moisture on the skin only aggravates a hot situation. Light, breathable, moisture-wicking garments work best, and these days they aren't difficult to find. Just peruse any hunting retail store or catalog and you'll find everything you might need.

Some summer hunters venture afield in nothing more than shorts and a T-shirt topped with a mesh bug suit. A baseball-style hat is recommended to help shade the face, but try to use one with mesh on the back to promote air circulation.

The summer months can offer some great hunting if you take the proper steps to stay comfortable. (Larry Teague)

Temperatures in the late summer months can be downright unbearable at times. Be careful to keep your body fully hydrated and as cool as possible. Drinking plenty of water or sports drinks will help ward off health problems, but try to avoid caffeine drinks, which act as diuretics that dehydrate the body. In addition, eat very little, if anything (being sensible, of course). Eating is like throwing a log on the fire, causing the body to raise its temperature as it breaks down and distributes nutrients.

TACTICS FOR HUNTING IN HOT WEATHER

Hog hunters must adapt to changing conditions in the summer months. Hogs may shift their home range or habits slightly to adjust to new conditions. For example, swamps may dry up in places, food sources may be in different locations, and other sources of water may draw animals to new areas.

STAND HUNTING

The primary concern of a hog is always to fill his belly, and this should be taken into consideration. Hunting over a natural food source can range from unbelievable to very unpredictable. It all depends on whether food is widely distributed or very localized.

The perfect situation is to have only a few select food sources available. Unfortunately for the summer hunter, this scenario is a bit tougher to find than it is in the fall and winter, when only a handful of trees with hard or soft mast may be producing. Summer food sources are usually more stable, as they don't change with frost and other weather conditions.

One good area to hunt in late summer is around a farmer's garden or fields. Hogs often visit freshly plowed fields early in the summer to scour the soft, upturned earth for fresh, tender roots. Later in the summer, as crops start to mature, these fields and gardens are again hog havens. Farmers are usually only too happy to allow you access to thin out the local wild hog population.

Another key food source worth watching is the edge of a healthy grass meadow. Vegetation is concentrated and easy to obtain in these spots, so hogs will certainly show up eventually.

BAIT HUNTING

As discussed earlier, bait hunting is productive year-round, but it's much more predictable than any natural source of food during the summer. Hunters who position themselves over a bait source during the last hours of daylight nearly always find more success than those who sit on natural foods that may only be used sporadically at this time of year.

Patience is the key, and this seems to be even more applicable during very hot days, when a herd may be reluctant to move until just before or after dark. As with most game animals, hog movement peaks during the last hours of daylight, with some activity taking place throughout the night and into the first hours of morning. Fortunately for the summer hunter, these are also the most comfortable times of day. During the heat of the day, a hog will spend the bulk of its time in the coolest spot it can find, preferably in the shade and/or the mud, which helps deter bugs.

My success over bait, or any food source, for that matter, during morning hunts has been minimal. In fact, I have only seen hog movement an average of one out of every ten mornings while hunting over bait. This is incredibly low compared to my average of seven out of ten during evening hunts.

For the most part, hogs are nocturnal. They feed intermittently throughout the night, and by morning they're ready to bed down. The only stop they might make to feed at this time will be on the way to the bedding area, which may shift slightly during the summer. It generally stays within an area of a couple hundred yards, depending on the terrain.

I highly recommend hunting over bait during the evening hours, but I usually try a different tactic during morning hunts.

STILL-HUNTING

One tactic that can be very productive during the morning hours and throughout the day is still-hunting. Slipping quietly through known bedding areas can also lead to some excitement.

Many hunters prefer to still-hunt during the summer months because hogs are sometimes reluctant to move, and when they do it isn't usually very far. Unless they are conditioned to a feeder of some kind, it's tough to pin down their movements enough to have much confidence in a stand hunt. Too much food is usually available throughout their habitat at this time.

But for the still-hunter, this unpredictable movement by the hogs can come in handy. They may turn up

Summer hunting is also a great way to keep your skills sharp for deer season.

Year-Round Hunting

in many more locations to mill about while feeding or rooting, and it may be easier to mask your approach.

A hog's first line of defense is sense of smell, followed by hearing, and then eyesight. Still-hunters should hunt into the wind and be very conscious of any shift in wind direction, as smells are distributed more widely in the heat. Total scent elimination is nearly impossible at this time of year.

Once you're in a productive area, move very deliberately. Although a hog's eyesight isn't as keen as that of some other animals, they readily perceive movement and can quickly discern the shape of a man, unless it's broken up well. Hunt meticulously through areas known to contain hogs, stopping every few steps to study the terrain and cover and to listen intently for any sound that may give away a hog's location. Hogs can be extremely vocal at times, which will quickly become evident in areas that hold high concentrations of porkers.

Success rates among still-hunters can be very high during the summer, and it is the only method, with the exception of hunting with hounds, that is effective when hogs seem to be moving mostly at night.

HOT-WEATHER GAME CARE

At no time is the fruit of your hunting labor more vulnerable than during the hottest days of the year. Many hunters refuse to go afield in the summer for this reason, but if the hunter is expedient in caring for his meat, the result can be a freezer full of great-tasting pork.

Of course, quick action shouldn't be reserved only for hot days, but it is certainly more important at this time. First, it's critical to make a quick, clean kill. This should always be the hunter's goal, but from late fall through early spring a hit in late evening, if need be, can be followed up the next morning. But

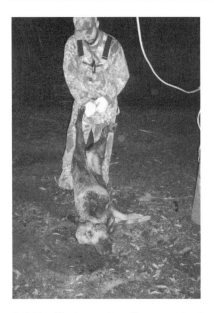

Quickly skinning and cooling an animal is the key to keeping the meat tasty after a hot-weather hunt.

this certainly isn't the case from late spring to early fall, where nighttime temperatures may stay above 70 degrees.

An animal left overnight during the warmer months will probably be spoiled by morning, or will be questionable at the very least. It simply isn't worth the health risk to leave an animal in the field for hours. To avoid this, a hunter must be very disciplined, taking only sure shot opportunities that are likely to drop an animal in its tracks.

This isn't too difficult for most rifle hunters, but bowhunters have a tougher time, even with a solid hit. An animal that has been hit well may still travel several hundred yards before expiring. Archers can benefit greatly by adding a Game Tracker to their tackle.

A Game Tracker is a canister filled with a string, similar in strength and texture to dental floss, which mounts directly to the bow. The string is then attached to the arrow. On the release, string feeds out smoothly, allowing the hunter to quickly track the animal simply by following the string. With this device, it no longer matters whether or not there's a blood trail to follow. I particularly recommend it for summer hunting, although it can serve the bowhunter equally well year-round.

After recovery, a hog should be field dressed on the spot and the incision propped open to allow proper circulation of the carcass. Waste no time in skinning, quartering, and placing the meat in an ice-filled cooler.

For summer hunts—or anytime insects might quickly gather on a dispatched animal—it can be very helpful to carry a small spray bottle filled with a solution of citric acid. Food-grade citric acid can be purchased at most pharmacies or feed stores, and it helps slow bacteria growth, which is the primary culprit in meat spoilage. It is also very effective at deterring pesky insects. About two ounces of citric acid to one quart of water should do the job. Spray the meat liberally, but still try to get it out of the woods and in the freezer quickly.

Summer hunting for hogs can become nearly as addictive as hunting at any other time of year. It's a great way to keep your hunting skills sharp, and it takes the edge off waiting the long months until the general big game season starts. Summer certainly isn't the most comfortable time to be hunting in most hog habitat, but short outings of a few days here and there will keep you busy until those first frosty mornings arrive.

Chapter
6

SOUTHERN HOGS

"Don't leave your stand for any reason," said Mike Stroff, owner of Black River Plantation, as we approached my stand on the edge of a backwater slough. To strengthen his first remark, he added, "Everything out here will bite." As we had just traveled at least a half-mile into the Black River Swamp in his eight-wheeled all-terrain vehicle (an Argo), I wasn't about to argue.

Located in the low country of South Carolina, the Black River Swamp is home to a variety of critters, including alligators and snakes. But wild hogs don't seem to mind these menaces; in fact, they seemed right at home in the muck and black water, even devouring the occasional water moccasin.

Hogs are well suited to swamp life, enjoying the coolness of the mud and resisting snakebites with their tough, armor-like skin. Also, secluded swamps allow them to go about their daily routine without interruptions.

I climbed into my perch and watched as my only ticket out of this place rounded the last bend toward high ground. My mind began to wander through the list of slithering creatures that could

This vehicle offered the only way out of the swamp, where hog hunting was at its best.

possibly climb into the stand with me. I snapped to attention at the slightest of sounds. For a country boy from the mountains, the swamp scenery was surreal.

Once the commotion created by our arrival diminished, the swamp seemed to come alive. The hoots of numerous owls, along with the high-pitched cackle of a crane, kept my ears busy. I watched as a water moccasin slithered along the sunken roadbed leading to the stand. I was grateful for the sixteen vertical feet that separated us. I settled in and tried to enjoy all of God's creations, no matter what their form.

I hadn't been there long when hog sounds reached my ears, quickly growing louder. The easily discernible sounds that only wild pigs make were proof of what Stroff had already relayed to me—there were plenty of hogs in the area. Soon the splashing sounds and squeals were very close; the animals were just out of sight in the heavy undergrowth.

As a few small pigs began to file out of the palmettos one at a time, I anticipated the boar I knew had to be with the group. The hogs quickly found a dry spot and began to feed on roots and tubers. Among them were a large calico sow, a much larger black boar, and seven smaller pigs. The black boar certainly got my attention, as I was looking for a trophy. He had gray whiskers along his lower jaw and long tusks that would have been a great addition to any trophy room.

As I watched the group root along in the muck, I was still in a quandary about which hog to target. Although the boar was much larger than the sow, I wasn't completely sure I wanted to shoot him. If that doesn't make much sense, you must understand that once a hog, particularly a boar, exceeds two hundred pounds the tastiness associated with wild pork begins to diminish, sometimes significantly. So the sow would eat much better while the boar would look better on the wall.

After only brief contemplation, I shouldered my Knight .52-caliber muzzleloader. Taking careful aim, I placed the crosshairs just behind the hog's shoulder. At the report of the muzzleloader, all the hogs hastily made their way to cover, except one—the calico sow. Good sense had won out over the desire for a trophy. I had chosen the sow because of the high-quality eating it would later provide.

I passed up numerous other hogs before settling on this sow.

WHAT TO EXPECT IN THE SOUTHEAST

The above hunt took place slightly more than an hour inland, and it was a classic southeastern hunt. I was fortunate in that I didn't have to travel far from home to find plentiful hogs. This was also a prime example of a "sleeper area" for hog hunting.

Though South Carolina is well known for many types of hunting, hog hunting isn't among them. This is probably due to the fact that hog populations are very sporadic throughout the state. Some areas don't have any hogs at all, while areas like the one I hunted are teeming with them.

Such situations exist throughout all types of hog country. There are several reasons for this. Weather and habitat certainly play a key role, as does over-hunting or even under-hunting where landowners own large tracts of land but allow no hunting.

The Southeast is notorious for severe weather. Drought or hurricane conditions can wreak havoc on the movements and proliferation of a resident hog population. For example, hogs love water, but when their home range is submerged they move on to different territory.

Hogs in this region can be found deep within a swamp or on the edge of a pine thicket or right in the middle of a palmetto patch. Any habitat that provides hogs with a feeling of security seems to fit the bill.

Farther inland, in what is considered the upcountry, the terrain turns mountainous with hardwood patches interspersed with soggy creek bottoms and lakes. The cover here is diverse, to say the least, and your hunting tactics must be varied, as well.

I have had the opportunity to hunt in all types of hog habitat, but I must say that my most exciting experiences have come

The massive swamp buggy is a common sight throughout Florida and other lowland states. Without them, it would be nearly impossible to access a lot of prime hog habitat.

within palmetto patches, where visibility on the ground is often less than ten feet. In these areas, I have actually walked to within spitting distance of several groups of hogs as they held tight in their beds, hoping trouble would pass without them having to waste the energy of getting up and moving.

In one instance, I was trailing a hog I had shot the previous evening when I heard a group of pigs approaching. Kneeling down to get a better view, I saw some piglets—probably less than a couple of pounds each—making their way toward me. When the distance between us was less than a foot, I reached out and grabbed up the calico-colored leader. The little handful wasted

Southeastern hog country can range from impenetrable swamps and marsh areas to steep mountain terrain.

no time in trying to summon its guardian with a loud series of squeals.

The mother, who was less than twenty feet away, responded with a grunt. Not wanting to open Pandora's box any further, I quickly released the piglet unharmed and made a hasty retreat to a more open area. God only knows what I was thinking.

These lowland thickets aren't the only areas that hold surprises. Laurel thickets or clear-cut areas, which are prevalent in more mountainous areas, can offer similar close encounters with hogs.

COMMON HUNTING TACTICS

Bait hunting and hunting near a natural food source are probably the most popular techniques in the southeastern states. The hog's favorite hard mast is the white oak acorn. If you locate a grove of productive white oaks, set up a treestand or blind nearby. Rest assured, hogs will be along shortly.

Many hunters maintain year-round feeding programs that offer a reliable food source for resident hogs. These hogs become very consistent in their patterns. But in years with an ample supply of white oak mast, hogs will readily walk past a pile of corn to get to this delectable nut. So no method is foolproof.

Another popular method in the Southeast is hunting with dogs. Hound hunting has a long tradition here. In North Carolina, Tennessee, and the mountainous section of South Carolina, hound hunters eagerly pursue both black bear and wild hogs. Most of these hunters are primarily targeting bears, but they are happy to take on a large boar. Hunters that target hogs almost exclusively usually operate in areas where bear numbers are very low or nonexistent and hog numbers are high.

Hunting near a food source is an excellent way to take a large boar. (Mike Handley)

HOW STATES CLASSIFY HOGS

North Carolina is the only state in the Southeast that considers the wild hog a game animal. Other states simply classify hogs as livestock, making them the property of the landowner on whose land they live. Florida puts them in this category. States like Georgia and South Carolina require no big game license for hog hunters. With the exception of North Carolina, none of the states in this region have regulations for bag limits or minimum size or hunting seasons.

Because many landowners consider the hog to be a nuisance rather than a trophy game animal, they often allow hog hunters on their land for free. And even when the landowner recognizes the sporting value of wild hogs, trespass fees are usually quite reasonable.

GUIDES AND OUTFITTERS

Finding an outfitter in the Southeast willing to take a hunter out after wild hogs is relatively easy. Most prefer to book combination

In many southern and western states, hogs are often hunted in combination with other game like wild turkey.

hunts when season dates allow, offering a chance at hogs, turkey, and deer during the same trip. But hog hunting has also become an excellent source of income in the off-season for many outfitters. They can now take clients out year-round, where in years past they were forced to find employment elsewhere while waiting for hunting season to roll around again.

FINDING SOUTHEASTERN HOGS

Hog hunting has historically been more of a hunt of chance; meaning that most hunters who took hogs simply did so while in pursuit of other game. This has changed in recent years, though, as several states in the Southeast top the list of hog-hunting destinations. It is no secret that the Southeast probably has more hogs than any other region in the country.

Many outfitters now offer hog hunts, and they are usually much more affordable than a typical big-game hunt.

Hog-hunting opportunities are abundant on many southeastern islands, but half the adventure is just getting there.

Florida is easily the most popular destination, followed by Georgia, South Carolina, and Louisiana.

Unfortunately, because most southeastern states do not consider the wild hog a game animal, it's difficult for hunters to get any firm statistics about population numbers and distribution. The harvest totals, gathered by state fish and game departments, that can be so helpful for whitetail hunters trying to zero in on productive areas simply don't exist for hogs.

Pinpointing distribution is further hampered by the fact that these animals can be very prolific in some areas, yet quite limited in others where habitat is overused. And legal, as well as illegal, transports and releases continue to take place on a regular basis.

Extreme weather conditions also push out or draw in groups of hogs.

Frankly, it is all but impossible to get a firm population count for this region. Any number given is pure speculation. Furthermore, because only North Carolina sets hunting dates and requires a big game license for hogs, even estimating the number of hunters who pursue hogs is basically just a guessing game.

Chapter 7

WESTERN HOGS

Hog hunting in the western states is basically limited to Texas and California. Though some populations exist in neighboring states, hunters hoping to bring home a tusker head to these two states and almost nowhere else in the West. (See chapter 10 for information on hunting javelina in the Southwest.)

It has been reported that more nonresident hunters visit California for hogs than for any other game animal, and many of these hunters come with nothing else on their minds. Hunters who travel to Texas, on the other hand, generally think of the hog as an additional opportunity, although as the sport grows in popularity more and more hunters are beginning to target hogs exclusively.

CALIFORNIA

WHAT TO EXPECT

Residents of California have enjoyed hunting wild hogs for several decades now. At a time when the landowners and game agencies of other states considered the feral hog nothing more

More nonresident hunters visit California to pursue wild hogs than for any other game animal. (California Department of Fish and Game)

than a nuisance, hunters in this diverse state were quick to recognize an exciting sporting opportunity.

California is one of the few states that recognize the wild hog as a game animal. But this is where the special treatment ceases. Though the state considers it a game animal, there is no set season, minimum size, or bag limit. The one requirement is that each hog must be tagged. Residents can pick these tags up for fifteen dollars each. Nonresidents pay nearly fifty dollars per tag, which must be purchased in addition to a basic nonresident license. Still, unlike nonresident tags for most game animals in western states, the number of tags is limitless—as long as the hunter has a pig to attach each to and the money to acquire more.

On the plus side, California is the only state where harvest statistics and hunter numbers are available. According to these records, in a recent year 44,000 packets of five tags each were sold to resident hunters (prior to 2004, residents could only buy packets containing five hog tags each). An additional 2,300 individual tags were sold to nonresident hunters in that year. As for total harvest,

43,000 pigs were reportedly taken, but according to the California Department of Game and Fish this number is probably very conservative because many harvests probably go unreported.

Public hunting opportunities exist here, but they can be difficult to find. As you might expect, hog populations and success rates are much higher on private land. Fortunately, because hog hunting is a popular attraction, there are plenty of hog guides available and fees are generally reasonable.

HUNTING METHODS

The most popular methods for taking hogs in California are hunting with hounds and spot-and-stalk hunting. Hound hunters are active throughout the state, and many come from neighboring states where it's legal to use dogs on other species like black bear and mountain lion. Just like in the Southeast, hog hunting here is an excellent way to keep a pack of hounds in shape while having thrilling days afield.

Spot-and-stalk hunting is a good method for California's open, rolling terrain. (Howard Communications)

The rolling, open meadows and wooded valleys and hillsides also lend themselves well to spot-and-stalk hunting. Early morning and late evening are usually best for this tactic. During midday, still-hunting often produces for the aggressive hunter willing to dive right into the chaparral thickets where hogs bed down. In these close quarters, shots will generally be quick. The hunter must be constantly alert to even get a glimpse of a hog, much less a shot.

Though baiting hogs is probably the tactic used by at least 50 percent of hog hunters nationwide, California is one of only two states with large hog populations that prohibit the use of bait; North Carolina is the other.

Hogs are widespread throughout the state, inhabiting nearly every county. The largest populations are along the central coast, within the Range Mountains. The terrain in this area can be very rugged, which allows cagey hogs to grow old, but at the same time it is ideal for the spot-and-stalk hunter.

At times, a hunter can see for a mile or more, something hog hunters in the Southeast can only dream about. At this distance, hogs may appear to be small dots, and the terrain may prohibit a direct or smooth stalk, but when a plan comes together the results can be nothing short of "hog heaven."

TROPHY QUALITY AND POPULATIONS

For the most part, California hogs don't reach the mind-boggling weight of those found in Texas and the Southeast. This is probably due to heavy hunting pressure in most areas.

Hog populations tend to fluctuate widely with the amount of rainfall. In years with very little rain, vegetation (i.e., food) dries up and hog numbers dwindle as reproduction slows drastically. Once rainfall returns to normal, hogs increase their numbers very quickly.

Western hogs don't usually reach the mind-boggling weights occasionally documented in the Southeast. (California Department of Fish and Game)

TEXAS

WHAT TO EXPECT

Ask any hunter who has been to Texas to hunt virtually any game animal and I bet he can tell you all about the hogs he saw. There may be no way to verify it, but I've heard it suggested that Texas is home to more wild hogs than any other state in the country. Considering the size of the state and the miniscule amount of public ground, this statement could easily be correct.

Unfortunately, as is true nearly everywhere, the state keeps no records of harvest numbers or the total number of hog hunters. Still, there's no doubt that Texas has an abundance of hogs. Nearly every outfitter that provides deer or turkey hunts will allow a hunter to take a hog at no extra charge.

Like many states, Texas is home to hogs that appear to be direct descendants of the first domestic hogs (left), as well as those more characteristic of the Russian strain (right). (Texas Division of Wildlife)

Whatever the actual population, Texas is well known as one of the top destinations in the country for wild hog hunters.

Texas has virtually no public hunting areas, but fortunately for the visiting hunter, many hunting ranches in the Lone Star State provide access to quality hog country for rates that often start as low as fifty dollars. They may or may not add a modest trophy fee for any game actually taken.

Don't confuse these opportunities with top-end guided hunts, as a premier whitetail hunt may cost in excess of $5,000, and on some of these same ranches a hog or exotic hunt may set the hunter back $1,000 or more. But these lower-priced hunts can get the hunter onto private land legally, and there's usually an excellent chance of bagging a hog, and, in some areas, a javelina.

HUNTING METHODS

The most popular hunting tactic in Texas is easily baiting. As most ranchers and outfitters strive to maintain an abundance of game on the properties they own or lease, feeders are usually in-

Many ranches in Texas allow hog-hunting access for a very reasonable fee, and it's often possible to take several hogs during a single trip. (Steve Smith)

terspersed throughout. This generally makes for some fat, delicious hogs.

Some hunters use dogs here and others still-hunt, but these tactics are usually limited to very large properties because hunters need a lot of room to roam in order to pursue either method with any level of success.

You never know what will show up in Texas hog country.

Hunting over bait is the norm in Texas. California and North Carolina are the only states that currently prohibit baiting for wild hogs. (Howard Communications)

OTHER HUNTING DESTINATIONS

While Florida, Texas, and California top the list of prime hog-hunting states, good hunting is available in many other areas, too. Several other states hold isolated populations that actually match, and sometimes exceed, hog populations in the "big three" states on a per-square-mile basis. Most of these are in the Southeast, but others in the Northeast and West can be found with some homework. States to focus on include South Carolina, Georgia, Alabama, Louisiana, Oklahoma, West Virginia, and Pennsylvania, among others.

If you're looking for something a little different, consider an exotic locale like Hawaii, which is fast becoming a popular destination for vacationing hog hunters. It's usually easy to convince family members to come along on a trip to the islands, and the hog hunting there is top-notch. In addition, certain areas in Hawaii offer other exotics such as feral sheep and goats or even wild turkeys.

The best method for obtaining information about hog numbers within a given state is to contact its fish and game department. Most state wildlife biologists are fully aware of any hog populations in their area, and because hogs compete heavily with indigenous game animals they will sometimes offer you very specific information about where to start hunting. Some may even have names and contact information available for area landowners who are complaining about habitat or agricultural damage from hogs. (See the appendix for a list of all states with hog populations.)

Oklahoma is a sleeper destination for wild hogs. (Mike Handley)

Chapter 8

PRESERVE HUNTING

During the late 1980s, at the young and energetic age of nineteen, I was constantly on the alert for new hunting opportunities. So after a fall big game hunting season that was much too short, I began to search for game to pursue in the off-season. I was continuously flipping through the pages of *Outdoor Life, Field and Stream,* and any other sporting magazines I could get my hands on, always on the lookout for something new.

I eventually found a hunting preserve listed in the classified section that was less than an hour from my home. The ad offered hunters a chance to "hunt wild hogs in the mountains of North Carolina." The accompanying picture was of a razorback Russian-looking hog that appeared to be very agitated.

I was immediately excited, as I had never even seen a hog, much less hunted one. And the idea that I could do this just an hour away and return home that evening was unbelievable. The clincher was the price. It was quite reasonable, even for a teenager not earning much cash.

I had a lot of experience scouting for deer sign, hanging treestands, and using bows and rifles, but I knew nothing about hunting wild hogs at the time. After a brief phone call, and far too few questions, a date was set and my first hunt on a preserve was in the works. I didn't know what to expect. I had heard critics of preserves call them "canned hunts" for tame animals, but I kept an open mind and hoped for the best.

Shortly after arriving, I met two other hunters. One, an older gentleman, was also after hogs. The third hunter was there to hunt merino sheep. I didn't even know sheep were present on the preserve. The thought even crossed my mind to take a sheep if the chance presented itself, but I held firm; I had to have a hog.

We spoke among ourselves as we waited for the guide to arrive. Apparently, the older fellow had several hog experiences under his belt. I soaked up all his stories of hogs so tough that a 7mm magnum wouldn't take them down and of friends who had been rushed to the emergency room because they had been cut by a tusk as a hog made a fast getaway.

Being a hardheaded teenager, I wasn't ready to believe all these farfetched tales, but they did make me wonder, "Was it true, could a hog possibly be that tough?" I quickly pushed these thoughts from my head as we heard the guide's truck pull up. My mind returned to the day ahead. After a quick briefing about preserve rules, which included an extensive list of safety regulations, we climbed into the bed of an old 4 × 4 pickup and headed to our stands.

Once settled on stand, I looked down and signaled to the guide that I was all set. Soon the truck rattled out of hearing along the old roadbed. As the sky began to brighten, my mind raced. Things would surely happen quickly, as there were game-proof fences around us, plenty of animals inside, and a guarantee for success. It was a no-brainer.

Preserve Hunting

Sitting quietly, I strained my ears to hear what I knew had to be coming any second. After about an hour, I had heard nothing but one distant shot. As more time crept by without even a squirrel stirring, I began to realize that this was just like real hunting. The hogs certainly weren't running out to surrender, as some fellow hunters, who had never actually been to a preserve, jokingly said would occur.

My growing boredom was cut short by the rattle of the truck, which began to get louder as the guide made his way to my stand. As he pulled up, he asked, "What'd ya see?" My reply was, "Nothin'." We spoke for a bit, discussing the things that hunters normally talk about, and then he said, "Well, get in and let's go see if we can find those danged thangs."

The other two hunters I'd met earlier were already in the cab of the truck. The first to speak was the sheep hunter. It was his shot that I had heard earlier. He had scored, and his prize lay in the truck bed. He smiled as he told of the morning's events. Apparently, after a short stalk, the hunter had taken the larger of two sheep with one shot from his .30–30.

As for the other hog hunter, zilch. He hadn't seen anything, either. As it was nearing ten o'clock, we decided to return to the lodge, hang the sheep, eat a quick snack, and then return to the mountain. Although I hadn't seen any animals so far, I wasn't concerned. The contract I had signed prior to hunting stated, "no game, no pay," so I could simply return the next day if need be. Besides, I enjoyed the chase more than the kill anyway.

Clambering back onto the truck, we once again headed to the area the guide felt held the most promise for hogs. This time he placed us in strategic positions and pushed through a thicket that he was sure held a group of bedded hogs.

After less than thirty minutes of waiting, I heard three successive shots ring out on the adjacent ridge. I readied my rifle, sure I was about to get my first opportunity at a hog. Nothing.

I continued waiting until I heard voices nearby, then I began to make my way toward my fellow hunter. I found the old man smiling as he stood over a coal-black hog that probably weighed in excess of 150 pounds. He recounted the events like a child on Christmas morning. Evidently, he was nearly run over by the first two hogs that came his way. Jumping to the side, he quickly spotted another larger hog as it angled down the hill. The first shot was good, having entered just behind the shoulder. The second and third shots were evidently insurance shots, but they weren't necessary as he told of the hog stumbling after the first shot. Besides, only one bullet wound was found during skinning.

Now it was my turn. I was the only hunter yet to see an animal, and it was nearly noon. After gutting and loading the old man's hog, the guide and I headed to the lower end of the property where he thought the hogs he had just pushed from the thicket had gone. Slowly slipping into the area, we spotted movement. A quick look through the binoculars revealed sheep slowly meandering along a hillside—enjoyable to watch but not our game.

We continued on, making our way around the sheep and trying to avoid any disruption. It wasn't long before the guide once again motioned that something was up ahead. Scrutinizing the forest in front of us, I finally spotted three hogs at about a hundred yards, two black and one red. The red one was the largest and it was in fairly sparse cover, so I opted to take the shot.

Dropping to a prone position, I centered the crosshairs in the sweet spot and squeezed the trigger. The hog traveled less than thirty yards before succumbing to the fatal wound. We quickly made our approach, as I was eager to claim my prize. The two black hogs peered at us from less than fifty yards away as we stood over the rust-colored hog.

The guide glanced over at them and said, "If they come this way, grab a tree and pull your calves into the air, out of harm's way." The hogs seemed mild enough to me, staring at us and then retreating into the woods.

My first hog on a preserve was certainly no pushover.

Afterwards, I thought this fearful warning from the guide had been an act; that is, until he raised his pant legs to reveal several old scars along the outside of each calf.

Fortunately, my first experience with a preserve was a good one. Despite the poor reputation preserves are often stuck with, the truth is that there are many high-quality preserves and high-fence hunting ranches throughout the country. Still, some preserves with poor conditions or ethics do exist. Most of these are quickly weeded out, but it always pays to be careful. Always check a preserve out thoroughly before booking a hunt.

WHAT TO EXPECT FROM A HUNTING PRESERVE

Hunting preserves are, for the most part, very misunderstood. Some hunters talk badly about them, calling them "pen hunts" or claiming the hunting is only for tame animals. But in most situations this is far from the truth.

The Complete Book of Wild Boar Hunting

Preserves are just like any other business. Some are great, some are just okay, and some are downright horrible. The small group of preserves that fall into the latter category has tainted all the rest with an undeservedly bad reputation.

Getting the most from a hunt on a preserve is very much like getting the most from any other paid hunting opportunity. Do plenty of homework, ask the right questions, and if any red flags show up, just move on. Your investigation will include time spent on the phone with the preserve owner or manager, as well as with the references you should always ask for.

If an outfitter doesn't have time to answer questions or give referrals, there is no need to continue. Either his operation is of poor quality or he already has all the business he wants, which would be quite rare. Most of these businesses eventually move up in quality or go out of business, but enough fall through the cracks that you always need to be careful.

Here are some important questions to ask when inquiring about a hunt within an enclosure.

How many acres do you have, and what is the habitat like? There is no right or wrong answer to these questions. What a hunter must understand is that a twenty-acre enclosure filled with dense undergrowth where animals can hide will

A group of successful hunters on a preserve in Tennessee.

Preserve Hunting

probably offer a much more sporting hunt than five hundred acres of flat, open ground.

I once hunted a small preserve in Florida for hogs and axis deer. The enclosure held slightly less than two hundred acres of ground that was filled with thick undergrowth. I was hesitant about going, as I figured a hunt in such a small enclosure would be too easy. I eventually decided to try it, allowing only two days of hunting time in my schedule. I figured I would be done in less than a day.

Prior to the first morning of the hunt, I was given directions to a permanent stand located in the center of a pine patch bordered by a swamp edge and a small one- or two-acre agricultural field. It looked like a piece of cake. I planned to be very picky as I had two days on this tiny piece of ground. Where could the animals go, right?

At the end of the first morning I had seen a grand total of one whitetail, and she was no tame animal. She carefully inspected the area, snorted, ran back to cover, slowly reemerged, and snorted again before finally leaving for good.

That evening was more enjoyable, as several axis and fallow does entered a larger field located at the edge of the enclosure and fed contentedly. But no hogs or bucks showed, at least not during daylight hours. The next day went similar to the first, and I left empty-handed. I knew there was plenty of game within the relatively small enclosure, but the excellent cover made them very difficult to find.

In my opinion, the perfect enclosure would be two hundred acres or more and contain a mix of suitable cover and open areas with a ratio of approximately 75 percent to 25 percent. In the East, when the enclosure includes a mostly wooded area of over five hundred acres, the high fence rarely even comes into play, beyond just prohibiting game from leaving the area. Eastern whitetail hunters can attest that although success rates are high and large bucks are taken in such enclosures, the hunting is no cakewalk.

In the more open country of the West, two thousand acres or more might be a good starting point, depending on available cover.

Most enclosures are managed well and carefully maintained; after all, the success of the business depends on it. If the animals aren't healthy and available to hunters, or if they escape the enclosure, the business will suffer. But occasionally animals do escape and others enter, which can also be detrimental. Most animals entering enclosures on their own are jumpers like deer, but hogs sometimes work their way under fences, too.

The type of habitat often dictates how much room you'll need to have a realistic hunt on a preserve.

When are the animals released? This question may seem a bit odd, but some game preserves actually release the animal to be hunted on the same day the hunt is scheduled to take place. Up until that point the animals are maintained in a small pen. Believe it or not, some preserves have even been known to release an animal as the shooter (notice I didn't say hunter) readies his firearm just outside the cage. Video footage exists to prove this, and it's the worst kind of canned hunt.

Though it is difficult for most game preserves to do, the best scenario involves stocking animals of both sexes and then allowing them to reproduce naturally, with only occasional new releases. This method produces the wariest animals, and the sporting aspect will be nearly identical to a fair-chase hunt.

Most hunting preserves that don't have the capability of allowing natural reproduction will purchase animals, and then immediately release them within the enclosure. Allowing the animals several days, or even months, to familiarize themselves with the habitat and terrain will allow them to become more adept at escape. Also, the longer an animal is allowed to roam while hunting pressure is applied, the warier it will become, which is desirable for anyone seeking a challenging hunt.

If you learn that the animals haven't been released at least a few days in advance, I would recommend avoiding that particular destination.

Is a kill or shot opportunity guaranteed? A guaranteed kill is generally the norm for most preserves, but it's not universal. The preserves that don't offer this promise often provide a hunt more similar to fair-chase conditions, sometimes with

Preserves are good places for new hunters to build confidence and gain experience for future hunts.

naturally reproducing animals. But this isn't written in stone.

What are the pricing guidelines? Some preserves offer a daily rate, which is usually on the conservative side. This price covers food, lodging, and guide service, and a trophy fee is charged according to the specific animal taken or an animal's trophy status. Many hunters prefer this arrangement, which allows them to take the time to view several animals before taking one that suits them.

Other preserves have a fixed price for hunting a particular animal. The shot opportunity is guaranteed, but if a reasonable chance is provided the lodge considers its promise fulfilled, even if the animal was declined, missed, or wounded. Most operations are reasonable about this, as they have a vested interest in seeing the hunter leave happy with the experience. But they understandably frown about missed or wounded animals.

Always have a clear understanding of how the preserve handles wounded game. Preserves often operate much like African safaris in that if blood is drawn the animal is yours, no matter whether it is recovered or not.

What is the source of the animals? Nearly all exotics on a preserve are raised on a game farm, and the same goes for hogs. But many preserves purchase their hogs from trappers around the country. These are wild hogs trapped in locations where large populations exist. The wild hogs are then transported to an enclosure and released.

Either scenario is okay, but I always prefer wild hogs, as they are usually a bit more evasive because experience and natural instincts have given them a fear of humans. Their senses also seem more acute. Given enough time, hogs from a game farm will eventually exhibit these instincts, as well, becoming smarter and shier. But truly wild hogs come out of the transport box this way.

What hunting methods and weapons can be used? Some preserves will allow any type of hunting the guest would like to do. This includes hunting over bait, stalking, or hunting with dogs. Others can only accommodate one or two methods. For instance, most are more than happy to have their clients hunt over bait, but many draw the line at stalking.

Some preserves refuse to offer dog hunting because of the risk of injuries to the dogs. Also, because many hunters who visit for the first time are greenhorns, they're more likely to freeze up when the action starts. This same hesitancy is the reason many preserve owners limit stalking, as well. They might not want game spooked from certain refuge-like areas or they may have another party out hunting or they may prohibit stalking simply for safety reasons.

Some lodges may prohibit the use of a particular weapon due to a bad experience in the past. These tend to be primitive weapons.

Find out about any other special rules, and ask for a copy of the preserve's guidelines. It's better to ask early on than to show up at a preserve that doesn't match your hunting style.

OTHER PRESERVE OPPORTUNITIES

Though most preserves heavily promote hog-hunting opportunities on their property, it's often possible to combine a hog hunt with other animals. Most preserves can bring in almost any animal in the world, provided a price is agreed upon up front.

Sheep and goats are probably the most popular secondary game animals for hog hunters. Typical huntable sheep species include the Corsican, mouflon, Texas Dall, Black Hawaiian, and merino. The Spanish goat, a slender goat with tall spiraling horns, is usually the top choice for this species.

All of these animals will vary in color and size, and pure strains seem to be a rarity, as a lot of cross breeding often goes into developing the largest horns for a given species. Most of the sheep are beautiful animals that are native to other countries, primarily in Asia. These exotics make handsome mounts and are delicious on the table.

While it's true that many of these animals are raised on game ranches, they quickly become wary after their release. And they learn very fast after the first shot is fired. In my opinion, no game animal is as wary or difficult to bag as the white-tailed deer; everything else pales in comparison. But in the right conditions, these sheep can give a hunter a run for his money, especially when the hunter is toting a short-range weapon like a bow or muzzleloader.

Many hunters who visit preserves, or hunting ranches as they are called in Texas, combine the hunting of hogs with exotics. If left undisturbed, all of these animals will become conditioned to a corn feeder. And they make great trophies that can be enjoyed for years to come.

Chapter 9

HUNTING HOGS AROUND THE WORLD

Hunters can sometimes be narrow-minded when the subject of hunting in other countries comes up. The United States has some of the best hog hunting in the world, but other countries can offer hunts of equal, if not superior, quality. Some countries strictly control the amount of hunting allowed, while others overuse or exploit their game resources. Because hogs have always been a great food source, the latter issue is especially prevalent in poverty-stricken countries.

Because hogs adapt well to a variety of habitats and food sources, they are present in one form or another in many countries around the world.

A handful of hog subspecies exist worldwide, but the most common (and the most hunted) is the same subspecies hunted here in the U.S.—*Suidae scrofa*. Several subspecies are considered threatened, which is the case with the pygmy hog; only 100 to 150 individuals are thought to still exist in Assam. Same goes for the Visayan warty hog in the central Philippines. Although

Wild hogs the world over tend to utilize habitat in much the same way. (California Department of Fish and Game)

both species are protected by law, illegal hunting still takes place, mostly by residents desperate for a meal.

Fortunately, strong huntable hog populations exist in numerous other countries. Australia, New Zealand, Russia, and Argentina are among the most popular destinations. For the less adventurous hunter who still wants to experience a hunt in another country, it's also possible to chase wild hogs in nearby Mexico and Canada, although populations are spotty. (Both countries have restrictions on taking firearms across the border so be sure to check the regulations before your trip.)

Most wild hog populations around the world were established the same way they were in the U.S.—by escapees from domestic hog populations. And just like almost all of our state fish and game departments, many countries feel that high hog populations can be detrimental to local habitat. On some islands, the wild hog has been blamed for the annihilation of many indigenous plant and animal species through direct predation or habitat destruction.

It has been stated by some wildlife biologists that the feral pig is possibly the most significant mammalian pest of agriculture. (Apparently these naysayers have never chased after a pack of bellowing hounds or made a successful stalk on a group of hogs.) Due to this fact, many countries welcome hog hunters;

Just like in the U.S., most wild hog populations in other countries originated from escaped domestic livestock, and wildlife managers are often just as anxious to keep their populations in check.

some don't even charge a fee for a license. But some of these countries are beginning to recognize the positive economic impact that hunting, even for feral hogs, has to offer.

Because the hogs most commonly hunted in other countries are the same subspecies as the ones found in the U.S., most of the same hunting techniques are effective. For example, in Australia and New Zealand hunting with dogs is a highly regarded sport. In many South American countries—with Argentina probably the most highly regarded—spot-and-stalk hunting is a common practice.

Hog-hunting tactics are basically the same everywhere. Local terrain will dictate the best method. (Howard Communications)

The major differences in hunting these other countries are the varying cultures and game management practices. The rest is plain hog hunting. You should always remember three simple rules no matter what the hog-hunting destination: (1) The hog's sense of smell is the same everywhere, very keen and relied upon above all else; (2) If hunted in an ethical manner, hogs will always provide plenty of excitement; (3) When properly prepared, hogs the world over are great on the dinner table.

HOG HUNTING OUTFITTERS AROUND THE WORLD

What follows is a compilation of various outfitters around the world that specialize in hog hunting. Some of these outfitters have been in business for several generations, others a much shorter time. Simply being in business isn't validation of a quality hunting experience, though, which is why references are always recommended. Simply put, if you get a bad vibe from one company, continue trying until you find the right outfitter in your country of choice.

These days, it's also possible to do a lot of research on the Internet. The list below should provide a starting point, but don't hesitate to go online to pull up additional information on these or other outfitters.

Australia and New Zealand

Australia Wide Safaris
P.O. Box 2121
Humpty Doo NT, 0836
Australia
61–889–788–959

Buffalo Safaris
Owen Davies
Box 488
Beechworth, 3747
Australia
613–572–82097

Havago Hunting
Jim and Debbie Deickmann
Millmerran 4357
Australia
61–746674152

Doughboy Safaris
Alex Monahan
30 Hampden Street
Murchison, New Zealand
64–3–523–9249

LJ Hunts Australia
Len James
7 Moss Street Melton South
Melbourne, 3338
Australia
0427201260
or 61397479087

Hunt New Zealand Safaris
John Berry
Lawford Road RD5
Christchurch, New Zealand
64–3-349–5842

Deep South Hunting
Jim Landreth
33 Kinmont Crescent
Mosgiel, New Zealand
64–3489–4890

Kiwi Safaris New Zealand
Mike Freeman
Box 27–079
Christchurch
New Zealand
64–3384–4311

Canada and Mexico

Hog Wild Specialties
Deb Hagman
Box 1209
Mayerthorpe, Alberta
Canada   TOE 1NO
780-786-4629

Rancho Los Apaches
Frank Salido
720 Dellwood Drive
Laredo, Texas 78045
956–717–0883

Europe

Carpatica Hunt
Printz Alexandru
Bucharest, 098061
Romania
4021–7252107 or
40722–577929

Ay-Fi Safaris
Maltepe 06570
Ankara, Turkey
90–312–232–4820

euroHunters
Yourii Ostrokon
Office 1, 6 Kanarche Street
Darvenitsa, Sofia
Bulgaria
359–88–8522653

South America

Argentina Big Hunting
Patrick Geijo
5N022010 "A"
LA Plata, Argentina

MG Hunting
Marcelo Gil
Av. Libertador 2642
Olivios—PCIA
Buenos Aires, 1636
54–11–4794–6913

Hucal Safaris
Pablo Rossi
Fuerte Argentino 595
Buenos Aires, Argentina
54–291–4541905

Hunting Chile
Carlos Hernandez
Ingeniero Pedro Blanquier
6280 Las Condes
Santiago, Chile
56–2–2114130

Chapter 10

JAVELINA

Just like the prickly pear and the pitchfork-shaped saguaro cactus, the javelina is one of the most recognizable symbols of the Southwest. This little pig has a grizzled black and gray coat with a white collar across the back and just forward of the shoulders. It's also known as the collared peccary.

Each year more than 60,000 hunters head to the field in pursuit of javelina. Of that number, approximately 25,000 are successful. That equates to a pretty high success rate, even though many hunters can't or won't put in the footwork necessary to hunt well or only spend a couple of days hunting each season. The devoted hunter's odds for success are much higher.

The total javelina population in the Southwest exceeds 250,000. While Texas can lay claim to the highest resident population, Arizona has the largest population accessible on public land. (Roughly 70 percent of Arizona is public land, versus almost none in Texas, where most hunting is done on private leases.)

RANGE AND DISTRIBUTION

In the U.S., javelina inhabit Arizona, New Mexico, and parts of Texas. Their range is limited to arid desert country, as they have no underlying fur to help stave off severe cold. Research suggests that the javelina first moved into the Southwest during the late 1600s and early 1700s.

Their earlier range was northern South America, and they migrated north from there. Relatives of the javelina, such as white-lipped peccary and the chacoan peccary, continue to thrive in South America.

WILD HOG RELATIVES?

The wild hog and javelina share some traits, including general appearance and habits, but they are only distantly related. Still, they are hunted in similar ways, and chasing javelina is just as addictive as wild hog hunting.

Javelina are distant relatives of the wild hog, but they have some unique characteristics. (Texas Wildlife and Parks)

These animals share the same order, but belong to separate families. Hogs are in the Suidae family, while javelina belong to Tayassuidae. These scientific classifications really don't mean much to the average hunter, but it's still interesting to know that javelina aren't actually hogs as we know them.

HABITS

Like the wild hog, javelina are very gregarious. They typically travel, eat, and sleep in groups. Each year, hunters come out of the field with stories of seeing forty-plus javelina together. It's certainly possible, but a lot depends on hunting pressure, availability of food, and the population in a given area. A study completed by the Arizona Game and Fish Department found an average of 8.6 animals per group. That is a lot of eyes to hide from for someone trying to get within bow range.

Javelina are frequently observed rubbing against each other, and it doesn't seem as though any members of the group have personal boundaries they protect. Some of this rubbing occurs while "freshening up" a herd mate, which entails rubbing musk from a gland at the base of the tail. In addition to applying scent to herd mates, they also mark rocks, trees, bushes, and other structure in their habitat.

While javelina are normally peaceful animals, occasional fights occur for the same reason most other animals mix it up — breeding rights. Most groups aren't organized with a rigid hierarchy like that of a wolf pack; rather, a loose pecking order is usually determined by size, and there is no permanent leader.

The javelina is a very hardy critter. Of course, any animal that relies primarily on the cactus as a food supply has to be tough. And various cacti really are the mainstay of the javelina's diet. It may seem odd to anyone who isn't familiar with the desert environment, but most cacti produce succulent fruit each year.

Even those that don't produce fruit usually still have soft fleshy meat under a tough skin—the hard part is getting past those thorns.

SIGN

You'll find plenty of sign in areas with high populations of javelina. Look for the normal things when scouting: tracks, scat, and bedding areas. Scat is similar in size and consistency to that of a medium-sized dog. A lot depends on a particular individual's diet, though. If food sources contain a lot of moisture, such as when fruit is abundant or when recent rains have freshened up vegetation, scat will be shaped like a small pancake.

Scat dries quickly under the hot southwestern sun, so spotting moist scat often means animals are nearby. In the humid Southeast, this type of fresh sign is harder to judge. Be alert at all times, especially when sign such as this is found.

Because javelina prefer to travel in groups, tracks are usually easy to spot around water holes or in dry washes. This type of sign is obviously more difficult to find in areas with rocky terrain, so you'll have to look for other signs of recent activity, too.

Bedding areas are unmistakable, as the ground is generally raked clean of any debris by herd members preparing their single beds. Just as with wild hogs, javelina seek out thick, brushy areas for midday bedding areas.

FOOD AND WATER

One of the javelina's favorite foods is the prickly pear cactus, which is found throughout their range. They don't seem to have any problems consuming cactus spine. Prickly pear can be thought of as the white oak of the desert, as many denizens of arid country feast on it.

Other important foods include the cholla, saguaro, barrel, and hedgehog cactus. Javelina will also dine on the jojoba plant, which produces seed pods. A few of these plants produce fruit at various times of year. Non-fruit-bearing cactus are simply eaten, spines and all.

Javelina feeding sign is easy to distinguish from that of other animals that may frequent the same area. Tracks should certainly be visible, but the clincher is bite marks on the cactus. Because javelina have no chopping teeth, any cactus they eat will appear to be torn or mauled. Cattle, on the other hand, can bite through cleanly.

While javelina certainly like prickly pear, their populations in an area aren't tied directly to this food source. In fact, healthy populations have been found in areas void of prickly pear. And in some areas, they may only eat prickly pear when it's bearing fruit, usually in late summer.

There is still some debate about whether the javelina is an omnivore (eating both meat and vegetation) or only a herbivore (eating vegetation only). But several scat studies have indicated that a javelina's diet consists primarily of vegetable matter with only the occasional insect.

The issue of a javelina's water needs has also been the subject of some debate. Some biologists claim that they need water daily, while others insist that a hog can go for two weeks or more without drinking. A research project completed by University of Arizona professor Lyle Sowls showed captive javelina could easily survive up to ten weeks on the moisture and nutrients provided by cactus. However, after fifteen weeks without water—that's nearly four months—the javelina started to become weak.

If water is available, the herd may stop for a drink or wallow in the cool mud. But setting up your blind near a water hole isn't necessarily a great idea, because it may be days or even weeks before a herd returns.

Annual rainfall has a huge impact on the areas in which you'll find javelina. This is due to the green growth that occurs shortly after a rain in this parched country. Vegetation stays greener longer in local areas that get even a little extra rainfall, and the animals are quick to take advantage of it. Locate these areas in dry years, and you'll likely find javelina. If precipitation is widespread, though, all bets are off and the herds will likely be evenly distributed throughout the normal home range.

BREEDING

There is no clearly defined breeding season during the year, but breeding activity normally peaks between the months of November and March. The dominant boar does most of the breeding, and nearly all fights are related to challengers trying to assert their will.

Most javelina are able to reproduce at ten to twelve months of age, but many sows don't fully mature until around fifteen months. The oldest pregnant sow ever encountered was a hunter-killed twelve year old. Surprisingly, a study completed by the Arizona Game and Fish Department revealed that the majority of javelina litters contained just one or two piglets. Three piglets were found less than 10 percent of the time.

Piglets can travel with the sow just a few hours after birth, although mortality runs as high as 50 percent for young in the first twelve months. Mortality rates drop significantly once maturity is reached.

SIZE DOESN'T MATTER

Javelina are small in comparison to the wild hog. The average adult weighs only forty to sixty pounds, although an occasional specimen may approach the 100-pound mark. During a survey taken at various Arizona inspection stations, the average weight of 168 field-dressed javelina was just thirty-four pounds. This is what most hunters can expect.

What javelina lack in body size, though, they make up for with sheer spunk. Once fully mature, these little animals possess canine teeth longer than any predator on earth. And they aren't afraid to use them. Most will quickly charge in to help a herd member that is being attacked. Some credible reports tell of them facing and chasing off an attacking mountain lion.

Although not as large as wild hogs, javelina are tough little "pigs." (FWS)

LIFESPAN

The oldest javelina in captivity reached the ripe old age of twenty-one, while the oldest ever recorded in the wild was a fifteen-year-old sow from Texas. Hunters can age harvested animals by looking at the teeth. At twenty-one months of age a javelina will have all its teeth. Beyond that, a hunter can use the following data collected from a hunter's check station to get a better idea of age.

AGING BY TEETH WEAR

Type of Wear	Age
Only slight wear	2 to 3 years
Wear obvious on first and second molars, canines up to 1.5 inches	3 to 5 years
All teeth show wear; canines may be a bit shorter as wear is faster than growth	5 to 7 years
Very heavy wear, some teeth missing	7-plus years

HUNTING TACTICS

Several tactics have proven effective on javelina, and hunters are sure to find a method that fits their style. The most popular technique is spot-and-stalk hunting, with still-hunting and calling close behind.

Like many animals, javelina are most active during the early morning hours and again just before dark. During midday, they prefer to bed down under an ironwood or other shade tree. Within their home range, a specific herd of javelina will usually have between three and five bedding areas that see a lot of use. These locations provide good cover and protection from predators and are used year after year.

If you spot such an area while scouting or hunting, it will be unmistakable. There will be an abundance of javelina waste present, and the entire area surrounding the beds will have a distinct odor. It sometimes takes a lot of footwork to find bedding areas, but the results are usually worth the effort, as the group is likely to be somewhere nearby. Slow your search, and look for other sign in the immediate area.

GLASSING

Spot-and-stalk hunting is the preferred method of most hunters in the wide-open desert country javelina call home. More riflemen and bowhunters bag animals with this tactic than any other.

The usual approach is to set up in a good, high vantage point before first light and again before the last hour of the day. As the javelina's grayish coat helps it blend perfectly into the desert landscape, picking out animals while glassing can be very difficult unless a group is on the move. Looking for movement and their telltale color pattern is the key to spotting javelina.

Spot-and-stalk methods are usually best suited to the open, arid country of the Southwest. (Mike Handley)

Glassing is best with a quality pair of 8 × 40 or 10 × 50 binoculars. I prefer 10 × 50 because of the larger magnification. A quality spotting scope will also serve you well, as it's possible to thoroughly search the area surrounding a group for any unseen members that may thwart your stalk during those critical last few yards.

Sometimes you'll spot a herd immediately, other times it may take days before you find a group. But if you have done your homework, you will eventually catch a break. Two important elements of finding javelina are patience and footwork. The old hunter's adage, "deer are where you find 'em," certainly applies here, as well.

All hunters face the quandary of whether to stay put or keep moving. Game may appear as soon as you abandon an area, or you may move on to the next canyon and find it full of animals. Pick a strategy, be confident, and see it through. If your scouting has shown you that animals use the area regularly—and you have no reason to believe that they've been spooked—hang tight; they should be back within the week.

If you are the kind of hunter who simply must see what is over the next ridge, don't stop there. Spend time thoroughly glassing, then pack up and keep going. In game-rich areas, you will soon find animals.

Once you locate a herd with the binoculars or spotting scope, be patient enough to make sure no stragglers are hanging back. Then plan a stalk that puts the wind in your favor. A whiff of human scent will quickly put javelina on the run. And pay particular attention to the amount of noise you're making. Rhythmic footsteps or unnatural sounds, such as pant legs brushing against desert scrub, will spook javelina just as fast as human scent.

STILL-HUNTING

In flat terrain that holds thick desert vegetation, full-sized binoculars and spotting scopes are nearly useless. When your sight plane shrinks, a pair of quality compact binoculars will serve you well. Instead of spotting animals at long distances, the binoculars will be used to get a better look at shapes that could possibly be javelina. They can also be used to look into shadows where the naked eye might not pick out a well-concealed animal.

Javelina, like their distant relative the wild hog, primarily use their sense of smell for defense, but they can spot movement, too. Avoid showing a full profile or making any sudden movements. If you take these precautions, it usually isn't too difficult to stalk within easy bow range, provided an unseen member of the herd isn't bumped.

This is the most problematic aspect of the stalk. In most situations where cover is thick or intermittent, there will be more animals in a herd than originally spotted through the binoculars. There always seems to be an extra javelina tucked under brush or bedded down out of sight. Move slowly as you stalk, and continue to carefully scrutinize every bit of cover for that hidden animal.

CALLING

Many hunters feel that it's more exciting to interact vocally with game. From deer and elk to predators and turkeys, most game animals will respond to one vocalization or another. In the case of a javelina, the calling techniques are rather simple.

The most effective javelina call is the sound of another javelina in distress. Calling a javelina is similar to calling a predator, but the response is prompted by an instinct for group defense rather than one for predation. As mentioned earlier, javelina are usually quick to rush to the defense of group members, and the ones that come in are usually mature.

To call successfully, the hunter should make noise that sounds like a javelina being attacked. (Major call makers often produce such calls.) Initially, use about half the volume of which the call is capable. After waiting for several minutes, try again with more volume. If a herd is nearby, and they haven't been called to repeatedly, one or more of the members will come in on the run—so be ready.

If calling doesn't produce a shot opportunity, wait approximately fifteen to twenty minutes before moving on to try another area. Sound carries well in the clear desert air, and animals may be coming in from a distance.

Calling can be used in open terrain, but it seems to be most productive in areas with thick vegetation. A herd might be as close as a hundred yards but well hidden in the brush to one side of a hunter's line of travel. They'll definitely be within hearing range, although you won't be able to see them.

TROPHY HUNTING

As with hunting of any type, the hunter who spends several seasons in the field will eventually find himself pursuing only trophy animals. Because there are no antlers to judge, trophy quality among javelinas is determined much like it is for bear or mountain lion. The overall length is added to the overall width, and the score is the sum of the two.

Though javelina aren't recognized by organizations like Boone & Crockett or Pope & Young, other groups in the Southwest do keep records. Most of these are state agencies or area clubs that may pursue javelina exclusively.

Spotting a trophy can sometimes be difficult for the novice javelina hunter. Experience, which comes from observing a lot of animals, will make this task easier. Still, there are a few guidelines that will allow neophytes to pick out mature animals.

Two key elements when choosing a trophy are age and gender. As with most other game, males will be larger than females and older animals will usually be larger than younger ones.

Differentiating between the genders is sometimes difficult. Boar skulls are generally shorter and wider than sows, so if a javelina has a blocky-looking head it's probably a boar. Also, if a herd is moving undisturbed a sow will usually be in the lead, while the largest boar will take up the rear.

An excellent way to pick out animals that are over two years of age is to look closely at the knees. Older animals will have little, if any, hair in this area, and calluses will be present from kneeling down while rooting. To use the latter method with any effectiveness, the hunter must be able to see most, if not all, of the herd.

In many situations, you can simply choose the animal that appears to be the largest. More likely than not, this will be the oldest male in the herd.

Regardless of how large individual animals may be, javelina are thrilling to hunt and excellent on the grill. They also make wonderful trophies, from a life-sized mount to a skull mount and anything in between.

Be careful, though, as most hunters find javelina hunting very addictive. You may soon find yourself canceling the family vacation to find funds for your next javelina hunt. If your family doesn't understand, just take them along. After seeing the beautiful scenery and animals and experiencing the challenge of the hunt, they'll soon see it your way.

Chapter 11

WARTHOGS

Hunting the wild hog anywhere is exciting and fun, but chasing its cousin the warthog in exotic African locales takes things to a new level. A different continent and country, habitat like no other in the world, and the sense of adventure that comes with hunting somewhere completely new combine to create one of the most exciting hunts on earth. Traipsing through the lush tall grasses of South Africa while constantly on the lookout for the telltale sign of an escaping warthog is an experience every hog hunter should have at least once.

Nearly everything in the African bush has horns, thorns, or fangs, which makes stalking through thick vegetation particularly unnerving. At times, it's only possible to see twenty paces or less in front of you, and there's no telling what's around the next bush. This is Africa, after all, and humans aren't always at the top of the food chain here.

The excitement of visiting the Dark Continent brings some hunters back time and again. For the average hunter, though, it may take a lifetime of saving pennies to afford that dream trip. Either way, it's worth it to see this fantastic continent and hunt the wild warthog.

CHARACTERISTICS AND HABITS

The warthog is an African pig, with traits very similar to our feral or Eurasian version, although with a few minor differences. Much like the wild boar, the warthog will forage daily and can be encountered at any time. And they readily kneel to the ground and root with their tusks when searching for food, often turning up the ground like a rototiller.

Also, at least once daily the warthog will seek out water to drink and mud for a cooling wallow and bug protection. This is sometimes followed by a visit to a nearby rubbing post. They have eyesight that is on the poor side, average hearing, and exceptional noses. Any of this sound familiar?

As to differences, the most obvious is appearance. Even to hunters who find wild hogs beautiful—which isn't all hunters, not by a long shot—warthogs are often considered pure ugly. And some hunters even concede that "ugly" is putting it lightly.

Tusks that stretch to ten inches are usually considered trophy caliber. (Wilks Hunting Adventures)

The first things you'll notice about the warthog are its amazing tusks, which have been documented in excess of a foot in length. In the ugly department, and as its name implies, warthogs do indeed have large warts on their heads. Most males have two warts on each side of the head, while females have only one per side.

Boars are noticeably sturdier than sows, and most boars have dark circles around the eyes. This is due to fluid secretions. Other aspects that differ from the feral or Eurasian hog include smaller ears and a body with hair much sparser than the coarse hair synonymous with hogs.

Warthog size is more similar, but weights in excess of 250 pounds aren't common, although they are possible. A large boar usually runs around 200 pounds. When mature, the warthog stands approximately thirty inches at the shoulder.

With its exceptionally long tusks, the warthog has been known to fend off attacks from lions, leopards, and wild dogs. Because of this prominent feature, or possibly a previous bad experience, many predators hesitate to even attack adult warthogs. There are documented cases of warthogs seriously injuring, and in one incident killing, a zoo caretaker.

While the chance of a hunter being hurt by a healthy warthog does exist, most such incidents result from approaching an injured animal without taking the proper precautions. If a warthog is injured during a hunt, the hunter should closely follow the directions given by the accompanying professional hunter (PH). The PH will usually have extensive experience with these types of situations and can reasonably predict the outcome.

When warthogs fight each other for breeding rights or dominance, the sparring animals are rarely injured seriously, despite those long, sharp tusks. In most encounters the attacker will run toward his opponent while extending his mane. The opponent then lowers his head and takes the full blow on his broad forehead, much like sheep butting heads.

The animals then press their heads firmly together and push aggressively while butting with upward thrusts of the snout, trying to upset the balance of their adversary. The opponents always seem to fight in a manner that prevents injuries to unprotected areas along the side of the body. Most warthogs make a constant growling noise during this shoving match, letting the other animal know that the fight isn't over.

As the tempo of the match slows, the warthogs may drop to their knees while still head to head and still flicking their tails in excitement. A match will usually last for some time be-

Despite their formidable tusks, warthogs tend to be mild mannered. (Mike Handley)

fore the animals separate by slowly backing away from one another. If serious injuries do occur between two opponents, it's usually because an inferior animal is cornered. As the lesser animal wheels around to attempt a getaway it sometimes hooks the other warthog in the side. This is really more incidental than an act of aggression, but accidents are bound to happen when animals run around with foot-long daggers sticking out of their jaws.

The warthog thrives from the dry, sandy country of southern Africa north to just below the Sahara. It prefers mostly open forest, with plenty of thickets for escape if trouble presents itself. These thickets make hunting for warthogs particularly exciting—you never know what you'll find lurking in the thick cover.

Most warthogs travel in small family groups. However, as with North American hogs, old boars often lead solitary lives. Sows may have up to six piglets per litter, but three or four is more common. As sows have only four teats, any youngsters beyond this number will usually die. Warthogs are omnivores, surviving on most anything they can find, including roots, plants, bird eggs, small mammals, even carcasses.

In sharp contrast to the habits of the wild hog, the warthog retreats to a hiding place once darkness falls, hunkering down until daylight returns.

Although warthogs are perfectly capable of digging their own burrows—they can move large amounts of dirt in a short time with their wide noses—they usually prefer to take up residence in the abandoned dens of aardvarks, sometimes even evicting the current occupants. These dens are very handy for the warthog because very little renovation is necessary due to the similar sizes and shapes of these two species.

Warthog habitat usually includes dense undergrowth that offers a quick getaway when the need arises. (Wilks Hunting Adventures)

Adult warthogs will actually slide backward into a burrow, facing outward. This allows them to face any would-be predators. Younger animals generally go in headfirst, and the last to enter is always an adult. The head of the adult warthog will almost completely plug the entrance, allowing it to fend off aggressors before they get within striking distance of the young.

The den is a safe hiding and resting place for the group, but it also serves as a nursery. During the mating season the boar will constantly monitor the stage of a sow's heat cycle. The mating ritual involves the boar circling the sow and making a noise that has been noted as sounding like a chattering motor — simply excited.

Warthogs don't make scrapes, but when a boar smells an area that has been urinated upon by the sow he will straddle that spot and issue a few squirts of his own. This is basically to lay claim to that sow.

Once impregnated, the sow will abandon the previous year's young and retreat to an area where no other warthog is currently living. After seeking shelter in an abandoned den, she will give birth and stay inside until the piglets are several days old, at which point she again ventures aboveground. At the ripe old age of one week, the young will begin making short jaunts with their mother. After three to four weeks the den is used only at night.

Most warthogs are sexually mature at one year of age and may live up to twelve years.

HUNTING THE WARTHOG

Anyone who hasn't yet had a chance to hunt the warthog is truly missing out on a great experience. Fortunately for the adventurous hunter, warthogs offer a bargain hunt in comparison to guided big game hunts throughout North America. While very few hunters venture to Africa strictly for the warthog, some do. In most cases, however, warthogs are an add-on to an existing safari package.

Because the habits and foods of the warthog are very similar to those of North American hogs, many of the effective hunting tactics are the same. Most outfitters offer their hunters the opportunity to spot-and-stalk, still-hunt, or sit on a waterhole. All of these approaches can be very productive, depending on the rainfall in a particular year or the local habitat.

The major departure from a normal hog hunt lies in the environment in which the warthog is hunted. The country they live in is often populated by a wide variety of curious and deadly animals, making almost every step an adventure in itself.

More hunters are now heading to the Dark Continent just to pursue warthogs, instead of taking them incidentally during hunts for more popular species. (Wilks Hunting Adventures)

Ron Porter, a taxidermist from New Mexico, is one of those few hunters who regularly travels to the African bush primarily in search of warthog. According to Porter, an outfitter he once used actually made the remark that while most of his clients ventured to Africa in search of the Big Five—lion, leopard, cape buffalo, elephant, and rhino—Porter was the only person he had ever encountered who came solely for the "Little Ugly." This doesn't bother Porter, though; he knows that hunting the warthog is a never-ending adventure.

According to Porter, one of the greatest challenges is getting within shooting distance of a warthog. Because of their height, or lack thereof, the only thing a hunter may see while slipping through warthog habitat is a tail being held high as a warthog makes his escape. In some areas, the understory can be so thick that the hunter must climb a tree to see a scant thirty to forty-five yards in any direction.

This type of terrain can lead to some surprises. On one particular hunt, Porter was slipping quietly through a thick growth of mopani trees, when he began to feel as if something was watching him. This can be nerve-wracking, to say the least. As Porter stood wondering what animal or animals could see him without being seen, he peered upward toward the treetops, where he quickly spotted his observer. A giraffe, whose body he couldn't see because of the thick brush, was staring right down at him from above.

During another hunt, Porter was following the tracks of a group of warthogs he and his PH had seen run into some thick brush. The terrain was rolling hill country, with grass just tall enough to hide a warthog. As they ventured ahead, keeping a close eye on the trail the warthogs had used, they spotted a herd of elephants just several hundred yards away. Most hunters in Africa agree that a cow elephant can often be the most aggressive and violent animal it's possible to meet. So the pair made a slow about-face, prudently retreating to look for warthogs elsewhere.

RECOMMENDED WEAPONS

Like their North American cousin, the warthog is physically tough, with a tenacity normally seen only in much larger African animals. It's like facing a wild hog that is twice as tough.

A bullet with less than 1,000 foot-pounds of energy can take a warthog, but it certainly isn't recommended. The same goes for archers who like traditional bows that don't provide a lot of energy. Hunters should always prepare for the common situation, not the perfect one.

Most hunters who venture afield in the African bush carry high-energy weapons, because there is no telling what might be encountered. But the best advice is to consult the PH or outfitter that you will be hunting with. Weaponry suitable for elk is an appropriate choice. A 7mm magnum with a 150-grain bullet might be a good starting point. The bowhunter should come equipped with the most powerful high-quality bow he can afford.

A MEAL FIT FOR A KING

One major drawback of an African hunting adventure is the inability to return with one's bounty. No meat may be shipped back. On the upside, most outfitters will gladly prepare meals from a hunter's harvest so they may partake right away. Most African game has an outstanding flavor, and warthogs are no exception.

Even the animal's hide must go through an inspection process before the hunter can take it home. It must be prepped by an authorized agent, who dips it in solutions that prevent any contaminants from entering the country. The skin must then be inspected and shipped through an importing agent in the United States.

Plan to spend thousands of dollars to take an African safari for warthogs and other animals. And if you decide to pursue any of the more prominent big game animals with your outfitter, you'll be spending even more. But warthogs and all African game animals make wonderful trophies for your collection.

CHOOSING AN OUTFITTER

As mentioned earlier, most established safari outfitters in Africa will help you harvest a warthog. Just be sure to let them know what you want during the planning stages, as most don't consider the warthog a species worth focusing on when there are so many other game animals from which to choose.

One outfitter in South Africa that definitely caters to warthog hunters is:

Jarandi Hunting Safaris
Andreas Jarisch
P.O. Box 13083
Port Elizabeth, 6013
South Africa
27-822-95-9521

Wilks Hunting Adventures
Rick Wilks
9269 Whitetail Way
King George, VA 22485

Chapter 12

FROM FIELD TO TABLE

Hog hunting doesn't end with the kill. Actually, this is when the real work begins, but if you handle things right you'll be able to enjoy the fruits of your labor during many a future meal. It's a good thing I like to hunt, because I also like to eat meat, much of it wild hog.

I don't claim to be a fancy chef, but I do know good eating. And I've never received a complaint about my culinary skills, as most of my friends are eager to lay hands on my homemade sausage or chicken-fried pork chops. So what follows is an accumulation of techniques and recipes for preparing wild boar that were passed on to me or learned the hard way. By all means, follow these directions but don't be afraid to experiment. You won't read about any hard-to-find ingredients here; this is simple down-home country cookin'. The directions are easy to follow, and the results should make a hog dog come running for miles.

FIELD DRESSING AND BUTCHERING

As hogs can be taken year-round in most states, hunts often take place in warmer weather. Between the months of March and

October, depending on location, extra care must be taken to ensure the meat from your kill is good on the table.

It's always important to take proper care when field dressing or handling any meat to prevent any possibility of disease transmission. Though the chances of contracting a disease from a healthy wild animal are low, it can still happen. Protect yourself by wearing rubber or latex gloves during field dressing—and this goes for any game animal, not just wild hogs. I like to wear latex hand gloves and shoulder-length plastic gloves designed specifically for field dressing. Always cover any cuts that you may have, as some diseases can only be spread from contact with an open wound.

How good an animal tastes on the table is directly related to how a hunter handles it in the field. Some insist that older animals, hogs included, will always be gamy and tough. A few hunters believe this so strongly that they won't kill an overly large animal, or if they do, they give away the meat. This is a shame, because it just isn't true. I have eaten young animals that were poorly cared for that tasted downright horrible. On the flipside, I have heartily enjoyed meat from hogs or deer that were fully mature or even old.

The determination of the quality of the meat you'll eat actually begins prior to pulling the trigger or releasing the arrow, and it continues until each meal is served.

A quick, clean kill should be the first priority of every hunter. In addition to being humane, it's the first ingredient for top-notch dining. If a hog is wounded but lives for minutes or hours, its body produces a mix of natural hormones. The best known is probably adrenalin, which helps the animal get away quickly and may even help it survive the attack. If an animal survives the attack this hormone has done its job. If not, it

Getting your animal out of the field quickly is the best way to ensure top-notch table fare for months to come.

simply creates a tougher cut of meat. So strive to make each shot count; you owe it to yourself as well as the animal being hunted.

Once the game is down, begin the cooling process as quickly as possible. This is easily done in cold weather, but becomes much tougher in the warmer months. A perfect situation would be to have the animal field dressed, skinned, halved or quartered, and in a cooler within minutes of the kill. I know this isn't always possible, but by just attempting to meet this goal you will be well ahead of the game.

MARINATE OR SOAK

You often hear about tenderizing wild game by placing it in a soak or marinade. Some of the recommended ingredients sound very good, while others seem outlandish. Buttermilk, Pepsi, vinegar, and salt water are probably the most common suggestions.

Many of these do work, but during a western hunting trip several years ago I found, quite by accident, a great method of ensuring that the game I bring home is delectable.

I had planned a trip to two different states, and after harvesting a deer in one state I packed up and headed to my second destination. I didn't have access to a steady supply of electricity, so to keep the venison from spoiling I alternated layers of ice and meat until the cooler was full. As I still had almost a week to hunt in my new area, the cooler needed to be checked daily. When the ice melted I drained the water and then restocked the cooler with ice.

When I returned home and began to unload my cooler I noticed that the meat was nearly white, any blood within the meat had been removed. Only a couple of days passed before I prepared steaks made from the hams. The venison had a very mild taste, almost sweet in flavor, which was better than any I had eaten before. I eventually tried this method with hog, elk, and a

Wild hogs aren't considered the prettiest creatures in the forest, but it would be hard to find a better-eating game animal. (Steve Smith)

variety of small game. It worked wonderfully. Evidently, this method also helps break down the meat fibers, much like traditional approaches to aging beef or venison.

Layer your hog meat with ice in a similar fashion, then leave it for three to five days. Check daily, adding ice and draining water as necessary.

Soaking half a hog can be difficult, but most coolers of at least one hundred quarts will accommodate a hog of average size. After the soaking or draining process is complete, the pork may be frozen or cooked immediately.

An excellent way to add flavor to the meat prior to cooking is to lightly coat the surface with olive or peanut oil. Then rub a small portion of your favorite seasoning onto the oiled area. Another marinade method that has become popular in recent years is injecting the cut of meat with a mix of seasonings, which ensures the entire slab gets an infusion of flavoring.

WILD HOG SAUSAGE

Pork has been used to make breakfast sausage for at least the last hundred years. And although wild hogs are a bit different than their farm-raised relatives, the meat is similar in that it is generally lighter in texture than beef or venison.

Making homemade sausage is a pleasure in itself, an accomplishment of sorts, as is any quality preparation of game that has been brought from the field. Making sausage can be a family affair, with each person assigned a specific task. In addition, preparing and eating wild game is often a great stepping-stone for getting other not-so-outdoorsy family members interested in venturing afield.

Any amount of the hog you desire can be used to make sausage, you will simply have to increase the other ingredients to match the quantity of meat. One thing to keep in mind, especially if this is your first attempt at making sausage, is that smaller portions are much easier to deal with. Larger amounts sometimes mix inconsistently. In my experience, it is best to start with one to two pounds of ground pork along with the other necessary ingredients. As you gain experience you'll get a better feel for your comfort level.

Generic sausage mixes are available at most grocery stores. Most of these can be combined with ground pork to create a tasty sausage, but using a personalized recipe allows you to create exactly the flavor you want. Perfecting a sausage recipe is very much an individual task. Some people enjoy very hot and spicy breakfast meats, while others like only a hint of heat or sage in their sausage.

By no means should you feel restricted to only the ingredients and amounts laid forth below; this is only a guideline. Other ingredients that are often used in small portions include sugar, lemon pepper seasoning, paprika, celery salt, ground ginger, or black pepper. Most of these should be used in amounts of a teaspoon or less.

Because sausage is made from ground meat, any cut can be used. Most folks prefer to use the lower shank meat, the rib meat, and any flank meat cut from the side area. If you need more meat than these areas provide continue with the neck and shoulders. Most game cooks go no further than this, reserving the rest of the meat for other uses.

My cooking plan generally starts with grilling half the hog on a large outdoor cooker at a gathering of family and friends. On the other half, I remove the chops for cooking separately, and make sausage from the shoulder and neck area along with the flank and rib meat. I usually smoke or bake the hindquarter.

MAKING SAUSAGE

1 pound of wild hog

½ to 1 pound of pork fat (Fatty pork shoulder or bacon, uncut or pre-cut, will work, but the amount used will depend on how fatty you would like the sausage.)

1 teaspoon salt

½ teaspoon garlic powder

¼ teaspoon dried sage

⅛ teaspoon cayenne pepper (This can be adjusted according to personal preference, but be conservative as even a sprinkle can be too hot for many people; if you add too much just add more pork to weaken the flavor.)

Combine all dry ingredients in a large mixing bowl, and set this mixture aside. Continue by cutting the pork into manageable chunks that can be evenly coated with the sausage mix; cubes of around one square inch seem to work best. Next, spread them evenly on a flat surface and sprinkle the dry ingredients over all pieces. After the pieces have been lightly coated, refrigerate the meat for thirty minutes or so, which allows the spices to saturate the pork. Finish by grinding the ingredients.

I recommend using the old hand-crank type of grinder, as there is no motor to wear out and they seem to work better than all but the most expensive electric grinders. Start the process with a medium plate on the outlet of the grinder. Slowly feed the chunks into the grinder until all have been pushed through. To ensure proper mixing, use a wooden spoon to turn the seasoned ground meat.

Now comes the most enjoyable part. Take a small amount of sausage and create a patty. Fry over medium heat. (I prefer to fry most meat in a cast-iron skillet.) Taste, then adjust the ingredients for the remainder if needed.

GRILLING OUT

Pork pull, pig pickin', hog roast—whatever you call your cookout will depend on where in the country you live. It really doesn't matter what you call it, though, because it's really about good eating and good company. Such gatherings are always enjoyable, especially when the bounty of a previous hunt is on the menu.

One of my favorite cookout recipes is what we in the mountains of North Carolina call a pig pickin'. The ingredients for roasting a hog are simple. And though the directions are easy to follow, too, an overcooked wild hog will barely be palatable. (This is true of most wild game.) On the other hand, carefully monitoring the pork will produce a delicious meal that will serve numerous guests.

You'll need one large cooker with an adequate amount of split wood for this project. I use a homemade cooker as large as some commercial grills, approximately three feet wide and five feet long. Some cookers this size even have wheels and a tongue and hitch to allow them to be hauled behind a truck.

Whether you're cooking a half or whole hog, it's much easier and quicker to cook it halved or quartered. Some spices and flavorings you might want to have handy include black pepper, salt, garlic salt, celery salt, onions, peppers, lemon juice, or even beer.

To begin the cooking process, build a fire from hardwood. Hickory is preferable, but if it isn't available oak is a good substitute. Keep the fire going for at least an hour, allowing it to burn down a bit and red coals to form, before placing the hog on the grate. Add a few more pieces of wood to the bed of coals just be-

Part of the fun of a group hunt is gathering around the barbeque to share good food and stories of the hunt. (Steve Smith)

fore putting the meat on. Monitor the temperature of the cooker with a cooking thermometer. The ideal temperature is just shy of 300 degrees. Regulate the temperature using any vents that may be on the lid of the cooker. If your cooker doesn't seal well around the lid, this task may be difficult.

Rub any seasonings you like into the meat, check the temperature in the cooker again, and then place the hog onto the cleaned grate. Leave the hog on only a minute or two, and then flip it over. Your goal is to sear each side, which helps hold in the juices. If the hog you're cooking is too large to complete this step with relative ease, simply omit it. But do it if you can because it goes a long way in preventing the meat from drying out.

Next, completely wrap all the meat with aluminum foil; a thicker foil works best for this. Again, wrapping helps lock in moisture, which is always very important with wild game. The hard work is finished for a couple of hours, so relax, watch a ball game, or socialize.

Cooking a half hog will take approximately four to six hours, depending on the weight of the hog. Remember to check the meat occasionally while it's cooking. After two to three hours, begin checking the temperature at the core of the rear quarter with an internal thermometer. When the core temperature reaches 160 degrees the hog should be done. Slice, or as we say here in the South, whittle, and serve.

BARBECUED RIBS

Killing a hog wouldn't seem right without cooking up barbecued ribs. Ribs are easy to make, and if cooked correctly they'll almost fall off the bone. All you need are ribs and sauce and a little salt and black pepper.

To begin, cut the ribs into portions that fit into a large pot of water. Boiling the meat will help ensure that it is tender.

After the pot is full, bring the water to a slow boil. Then reduce heat and cover. Simmer for twenty-five to thirty minutes. Try to avoid overcooking, as the meat will fall from the bone and become impossible to grill.

When the ribs are just minutes away from falling from the bone, remove, baste in barbecue sauce, and place on the grill over a medium heat with very little to no flame. I prefer a charcoal grill, as this adds a hickory taste. Add seasoning at any time. With the appropriate temperature, the ribs should be finished in less than six minutes. The meat should already be thoroughly cooked from boiling, and the grill is used primarily to sear the meat and add flavor.

SOUTHERN-FRIED PORK CHOPS

Other than fried chicken, no other food is more popular in the South than pork chops. Pork chops can be baked or grilled, but the most common method is to fry them in batter.

I have found it much easier to cut and work with chops if the bones are removed. Do this by cutting with a knife along the spine. Cut the entire length of the chop, all the way to the top of the ribs. Remove the knife and then cut between the chops and the top of the ribs at a 90-degree angle. Gradually work the chop free. Those more familiar with venison or beef will know this cut as the backstrap or filet mignon. Once it's free, cut the meat into ⅓- to ½-inch-thick chops. Then add your favorite seasonings.

Mix one cup of milk and one egg together, dip each chop into the mixture, and then lay it in flour. Coat each side generously and then place it into a preheated cast-iron skillet filled with about half an inch of peanut oil. Generic vegetable oil will work, but peanut oil adds flavor. For some serious southerners, only bacon grease is acceptable. The skillet temperature should be around medium. Cook until golden brown.

Another breading that I think is delicious on wild hog is House of Autry chicken breader. It is already mixed with herbs and spices and livens up any meat that is going to be fried.

CANNING

Canning vegetables and meats has a long history. It was used most often to preserve food in the era before every home had a refrigerator and freezer. The canning process allows food to be stored for long periods at room temperature. As some game meats, hog included, can be extraordinarily tough at times, canning is a good way to tenderize even the toughest cuts.

For bacteria to grow in stored food, it must have oxygen. During the canning process, heating and pressure-cooking the contents forces air from the jar by way of the edges around the lid, which seals completely upon cooling, preventing air from reentering. If the canning process is done properly the lid will have to be pried from the jar to reopen. You should hear a popping sound when you do this, a sign that the seal was perfect.

Any meat improperly canned or stored may exhibit bacteria growth. The contents should never be eaten.

It's possible to can food without a pressure cooker, but it may take you up to three times as long to achieve the same results. Therefore, the directions provided below are only for using a pressure cooker/canner and shouldn't be followed if you're doing without one.

Pressure cookers are available at most retail cooking stores. You'll also need several mason jars in quart or pint sizes—depending on your preferred portion size—lids and rings, and salt.

Begin by thoroughly washing the meat to be canned and cut it into chunks. The size of the chunks can vary, as long as they easily fit into the mason jars. Pack each jar to within an inch of the top, which will allow for any expansion that may take place. Add one teaspoon of salt for a quart jar or half a teaspoon for a pint. Some experienced canners recommend warming the lids by allowing them to sit briefly in boiling water. This supposedly creates a better seal. It's recommended but not required.

Place each lid onto the mouth of the corresponding jar. Then add the ring, which is used to help hold the lid in place. Snug the ring, but don't over-tighten. Doing so may cause problems with the seal. Place the covered jars into the pressure cooker and add water until the level of water in the cooker is about a third to half the height of the jar.

Turn the heat source to medium or medium-high and bring the water to a slow boil. Then attach the lid. Cook the contents for forty-five minutes at fifteen pounds of pressure.

Finish by cutting off the heat, allowing the cooker to cool for several minutes before removing the lid. Take a moment to ensure that the lid of each jar has sealed properly and that the rings remain snug. Store until ready to use.

Besides tenderizing the meat and allowing it to be stored for long periods without freezing, many people prefer this method because once complete, the contents are already cooked. Simply remove the ring and lid, warm the meat on a stove or microwave, and serve.

Chapter 13

TROPHY PREPARATION

A wild hog, javelina, or warthog can make an impressive mount. But to achieve the best quality, the animal must be properly cared for. This extends from the shot to the taxidermy shop. Most taxidermists can repair skins to some extent and hide some flaws, but severely damaged skins make poor-quality mounts, and in many cases can't be worked with at all.

Many types of mounts are possible with hogs. The primary options are shoulder, life-sized, and European mounts, but rugs are also something to consider. It's usually a good idea to determine what kind of trophy you'd like to have before even heading afield. This will enable you to take special care of the areas on the animal that will eventually be used by the taxidermist. For example, if you know you want a life-sized mount you should make the shortest, cleanest incision possible during field dressing. Or, better yet, if the taxidermist is close enough, make no incision at all. Instead, just get the hog to him as quickly as possible, and he'll take care of the rest.

Also, consider how you get your animal from the woods to the truck. If you choose a life-sized mount you'll need to closely care for the entire skin. So dragging your hog long distances is

Think about what kind of mount you'd like to have before you even take the shot.

not an option because it can sometimes rub off hair. But if you're planning only a shoulder mount, what happens to the back half of the hide doesn't really matter.

Although hogs are numerous and success rates are on the high side in most places, many hunters still go several seasons between harvests. And a boar that weighs in excess of three hundred pounds may come along only once in a lifetime. So always make sure you're prepared to take all the steps necessary to obtain the best-looking mount possible.

FIELD-CARE BASICS

No matter what mount you choose, most of the rules for proper care remain the same. What the hunter must realize is that when the trophy is subjected to harsh conditions—heat and moisture are at the top of this list—it obviously creates a tougher job for the

Trophy Preparation

taxidermist who is trying to preserve the prize. Many hunters don't give the condition of their trophy a second thought when they leave it with the taxidermist. Yet they always wonder why the same animal looks less than perfect when the mount is completed.

Field-care problems are easy to combat; the key is simply getting educated. Many otherwise knowledgeable sportsmen neglect to cool their animals properly. A lot depends on what time of year you take your hog. For instance, a hog killed in January in New Hampshire will be able to take much more abuse than an August kill in Florida. That is not to say that you should abuse either one, but some situations, as you will soon learn, allow more room for error than others.

It has been my experience as a taxidermist that hogs aren't the worst when it comes to slippage problems, but the smart hunter will care for them as if they were. Remove the skin as soon as possible to prevent potential problems, then freeze it or transport it to a taxidermist right away.

Proper field dressing will help your hog cool quickly, leading to a higher quality trophy on the wall.

A big mistake that many hunters make is hauling their trophy around to show to friends. This problem doesn't sound too serious, but you must understand that heat and moisture are prime breeding grounds for bacteria, which represent enemy number one to an animal skin. This detrimental bacteria begins to grow the moment an animal dies. It's nature's way of decomposing the flesh, something taxidermists are constantly fighting against. Even an otherwise properly cared for critter in nearly perfect condition can be lost due to slippage from bacteria buildup.

It is completely understandable why any successful hunter would want to show a trophy to his hunting buddies or coworkers, but your mount may suffer as a result. To avoid this problem and still be able to boast, take several high-quality pictures, go to a one-hour photo center, and then visit everyone.

Another common mistake that plagues many hunters is putting the hide into a plastic bag immediately after skinning is complete. If the hog hasn't been cooled properly prior to skinning, the skin will retain heat and may create moisture problems as it cools inside the bag. Place the animal in a freezer or at least in cool shade, without a bag, for at least an hour after skinning, then remove and double bag to keep other freezer contaminants from getting on your prize.

In the last chapter I wrote that the perfect scenario for achieving top-quality table fare from a hog was to go from live animal to freezer almost immediately. I know this isn't possible, but you should strive for this result whether preserving meat, the hide, or both.

WHAT TO DO IF A FREEZER ISN'T AVAILABLE

One of my favorite destinations for hunting hogs is an island off the coast of Georgia. Hogs are plentiful, but freezer space isn't. Anyone who hunts the island generally spends at least five days there, as transportation is by boat only. And many hunters take their hogs on the first evening. Dealing with this situation can be tricky, but a few specific steps will ensure that your trophy remains in good shape until you're back in civilization.

If a cooling unit or freezer isn't available it's more important than ever to remove as much meat as possible from the skin. Skin your animal all the way to the rear of the skull. If you regularly hunt where freezers aren't available you would be well advised to become proficient at head skinning. (Many videos and books describe the process in detail.)

If the hunter is familiar with this procedure, he can take along an adequate amount of salt. After fully skinning, he can simply salt the entire skin. If done properly this will hold a skin indefinitely. Otherwise, get the hog skinned quickly and place the skin in a cool area that offers good air circulation. After the skin is properly cooled, place it into a plastic bag and put it on ice.

Many hunters place the skin on ice without paying close attention. But if the bag has even a small hole in it the melting ice will leave you with a wet skin, despite all your earlier work. As mentioned above, bacteria thrive in damp or wet areas. Always double or triple bag your skin before adding ice.

CHOOSING A MOUNT

SHOULDER MOUNT

Shoulder mounts are probably the most popular choice for hog hunters. They take up very little space, and cost is minimal compared to a life-sized or half mount. Most shoulder mounts will have an open mouth, but closed mouths have been gaining in popularity recently.

To skin for a shoulder mount, cut around the girth or midsection of the hog, several inches behind the shoulders. Cut around the knees on the front legs, then make an incision up the back side of the front legs, cutting back to meet the initial cut around the midsection. Continue by skinning forward to the base of the skull, then sever the neck and remove the head and skin.

LIFE-SIZED MOUNTS, HALF MOUNTS, AND RUGS

For the sportsman with adequate space and enough money, a life-sized mount is a great choice. Life-sized mounts can be as simple as a rigid, standing pose on a plain base with a very small habitat scene or as sophisticated as an eye-catching action pose with an extravagant hardwood base filled with habitat material. For hunters who want a little something different, a lined rug with a mounted head is an excellent choice.

Skinning for a life-sized mount is a bit more involved than it is for a shoulder mount or rug. Your taxidermist may prefer that you make a ventral incision, which is similar to the cut you make in field dressing an animal. Or a dorsal incision may

Rugs have become increasingly popular. This one just needs to be lined with padding and felt to finish it off.

Trophy Preparation

best fit his work style. And then there is the rug cut. Contact your taxidermist before the hunt to learn which cut he is most comfortable with.

Many taxidermists like the dorsal incision, which is a cut that extends along the backbone from the base of the tail to the base of the neck or shoulder blade. This cut allows the taxidermist to avoid a significant amount of sewing. It also leaves fewer seams on the mount.

After the initial cut is made along the spine, carefully pull the skin forward as if you were removing a pair of coveralls, but in reverse. Most hogs require relief cuts on the back of each leg with this incision. This is easily done by cutting from behind the hoof up the rear of the leg to approximately the bend in the knee. Skin as close to the hooves as possible, then cut the bone with a saw or use a knife to slice through a joint. Remove the head and the skinning is complete. Keep in mind that a dorsal incision should never be used for a rug.

The conventional, or rug, cut is probably the most popular method of skinning for life-sized animals. With this approach, the skin will be useable for either a rug or life-sized mount. This cut may be a bit easier for the inexperienced skinner.

To skin using this procedure, begin cutting from just above one rear hoof. Cut straight up the rear of the leg about halfway, then gradually begin to angle the cut toward the center of the ham. Continue up to the body cavity, cut directly across the cavity, and then start down the opposite leg toward the hoof. Initially, keep the cut in the center of the ham, angling slightly back toward the halfway area, then cut along the rear of the leg to the hoof.

Make a similar front incision from one hoof down the leg across the body to the opposite leg, eventually stopping at the hoof. Cut from the rear incision to the front incision, and then cautiously complete the skinning process, being careful not to cut any holes in the hide. Hog skin doesn't peel as easily as the skin of other animals, so keep a couple of sharp knives handy; they'll dull quickly from all the cutting.

A short version of the rug cut is the ventral incision. It utilizes only one incision along the stomach area. This is probably the most difficult skinning method because the process is slow. The skin has to be worked slowly off each limb. Once each leg has been skinned almost to the hoof, and the lower leg removed, the remainder of the skinning process is like any other. An excellent benefit of the ventral incision is that any seam will be virtually invisible, as it will be along the underside of the mount.

SKULL MOUNT (EUROPEAN)

If you don't have room for a life-sized or shoulder mount, or if you just want something a bit different, a European mount may be the best option. Also, because most taxidermists use artificial jawsets, a European can be completed in addition to a regular mount. And if you don't mind making a smelly mess, you can even complete the European yourself.

A European mount is a skull that has been cleaned of all tissues and appropriately whitened. There are several ways to clean a skull: using dermastid beetles, boiling, or natural decay. Large beetle colonies can clean a skull in short order, but beetles are usually owned by specialty companies. Sending the skull to one of these companies is an option, but if you want to complete this project on your own consider boiling or letting nature clean the skull.

If you decide to boil, use a large pot and cook on medium heat. Try to avoid very high temperatures, which will only crack

Trophy Preparation

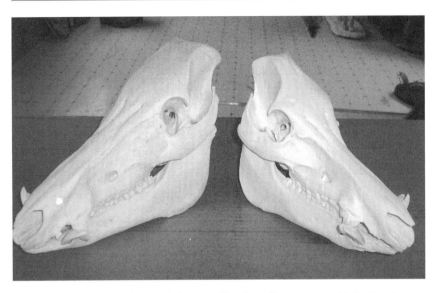

Skulls are a great choice for the do-it-yourselfer who still wants some kind of trophy.

or weaken teeth. Some people prefer to add a bit of Sal Soda to the boiling water. Sal Soda helps break down the tissues on the skull. Though helpful, it isn't mandatory.

As bad as it sounds, simmer the skull as you would a stew. Allow it to cook for at least an hour. Remove as much muscle and tissue as possible, then return the skull to the cooking pot. Most of the tissue will eventually release. The toughest area to clean seems to be the back of the skull. Finish this area with a knife. If stubborn tissue still remains, place the skull in a plastic bag and allow it to sit in the sun for a week or so. The excess tissue should naturally break down over this period.

Allowing nature to do the work for you has both a benefit and a drawback. The benefit is that the skull comes out exceptionally clean; the drawback is the smell. This method can be accomplished by allowing the skull to sit in a shady area or by placing the skull in a pot of water for a few weeks. (If it's placed in the sun the surface of the muscle tissue will harden and may prevent proper infestation and cleaning by bugs.)

The warmer months are ideal for the last approach, and of the two methods, I prefer to place the skull in a bucket of water. Allow it to sit for two to three weeks, then remove the skull and free as much tissue as possible. Change the water and replace the skull. After two or three more weeks the skull should be squeaky clean. It may not smell clean, but no tissue will remain.

If you choose to clean the skull without water, know that this process, depending on the time of year and location, may take four months or more. Place the skull out of easy reach of predators in a cage, staked to the ground, or tied to a tree. This method can work, but sometimes the tissue seems to get "baked" on. I know some hunters who actually bury the skulls, marking the spot and digging the skull up in four to six months. This works great as long as the dog doesn't dig up your stash.

Because hogs are naturally greasy animals it is best to degrease the skull before continuing. This step is optional but highly recommended. Depending on the grease content of a particular animal it may begin to "bleed" at some point, which just means that the grease is slowly leaching out of the skull and turning the surface a yellow color.

Quality degreasers can be found at most taxidermy supply houses. Coleman fuel will work in a pinch, but be extra careful as it's also highly flammable. More than one shop has burned down while a trophy was being degreased in this manner. Allow the skull to sit in the degreaser for thirty minutes to an hour. Then remove and let drain.

The last step to having a presentable trophy is the whitening process. Notice I said whitening and not bleaching. A liquid bleach is not recommended, as it will continue to break down

Trophy Preparation

Another option that doesn't take up much room is to clean and whiten the tusks and whets and then place them on a plaque or within a case.

the skull well after the bleaching process is finished. Most skulls that have been bleached eventually become chalky due to bone deterioration. If bleach is the only whitener you have available, mix it with water in a one-to-one ratio and allow the skull only a brief amount of time in the solution.

The preferred whitening product is commercial-strength peroxide, which can be found at most beauty supply stores. Use rubber gloves and a plastic or rubber apron when handling these products so you don't risk damaging your skin. Most come in strengths of 20 to 40 percent in cream (thick) or clear (watery). I prefer the strongest peroxide I can get, which is 40 percent. And most times I use a cream.

Simply brush the cream on and place the coated skull in the sun to speed the whitening process. After twenty-four hours, hose off the skull and put it back in direct sunlight. Repeat if necessary.

You can create a stronger whitening agent by mixing clear peroxide with dedusted bleach in powder form, which is also available from beauty suppliers. After mixing, generously apply the solution to the skull, and then place the skull in a plastic bag in direct sunlight. Hose off after a day and put it back in sunlight. Repeat if necessary.

Once the whitening process is complete you may want to seal the skull with a clear sealer or a light coat of clear gloss, but it's really a matter of personal preference.

Chapter
14

TIPS FOR SUCCESSFUL HUNTING

Whether you're a first-timer or a seasoned pro, hog hunting is much like any other undertaking. To obtain a maximum return you must make a maximum investment. For the hunter, this means allotting time to research, scout, and properly prepare for the hunt. And once the homework is done the hunter must stay completely focused in the field.

What follows are some key elements in successful hog hunting, or any hunting, for that matter.

ACCESSING QUALITY PROPERTY

When most hunters choose a hunting destination, the first thing they usually do is get a map of the area. Knowing the primary features of a piece of property is of utmost importance. But taking this a step further by identifying areas that are difficult to access or underutilized by other hunters may be even more vital to success.

We all know that hunting is usually best where pressure is least. When you peruse your maps of an area, remember that most hunters don't get more than a half-mile or so from access roads, either from laziness or fear of getting lost. Pick out areas that require some legwork to reach and you may find a "honey hole," even on land with a general reputation for getting a lot of pressure.

Also, those same lazy hunters may only hunt public lands because it requires no extra effort. It takes work to line up quality private land to hunt, and most hunters don't take the time to do it because they convince themselves landowners won't grant them permission.

The truth is, excellent hunting is still available on both public and private land. Either way, it's going to take a lot of work to find what you're looking for. But that is half the fun of hunting. If

Wildlife enforcement officers and game biologists can offer a wealth of information to the traveling hunter.

you neglect this aspect of the hunt, you'll spend most of your time in the field complaining about the lack of animals and the number of other hunters instead of enjoying exciting hunts for wild hogs.

PRIVATE PROPERTY

Accessing private property can be as easy as locating an area with a high population of wild hogs and then knocking on a few doors. Most private landowners welcome hunters who can help reduce the number of these prolific animals. High concentrations of hogs can be very destructive, so some landowners may even feel you're doing them a favor by taking several hogs.

Even when landowners ask for a trespass fee of some kind, it's usually very reasonable. Also, it sometimes helps to offer to pitch in on a few chores or to take along a member of the landowner's family who may have little or no hunting experience. A connection of this sort could lead to a lifelong friendship and a great place to hunt.

PUBLIC PROPERTY

Despite what you often read these days, some of the best hunting in the country is still located on public land. Unfortunately, finding these areas is the greatest hurdle. But once that chore is complete, you'll be able to hunt these places again and again. And you'll never have to ask anyone's permission.

Finding a prime hunting location will take plenty of research. You can check kill reports, population estimates, and so on, and then look over quality road and topographic maps before getting out and scouting on foot. Of course, because most states don't manage wild hogs as game animals, they often don't have the solid harvest statistics that normally help hunters zero in on areas with the best hunting. But you can bet that state wildlife biologists are aware of certain areas where wild hogs are causing problems, so getting the right person on the phone during your research calls may pay big dividends.

The best of these public lands may be remote or hard to access, though. Always look for unique ways to get to land that other hunters overlook or dismiss as too much hassle to reach. These may include going in by boat or bicycle or even asking for permission to cross private land to get to public hunting ground. Using any of these tactics will usually put you well ahead of other hunters who may not be willing to put forth this amount of effort.

LIMITED-ENTRY PUBLIC LANDS

Other public hunting opportunities that should be heavily researched are limited-entry areas. These can range from public-land, special-opportunity hunts like those in Florida to random hunts initiated on various state or federal lands where wild hog populations have increased to the point where herds need to be thinned before major habitat destruction occurs.

The latter hunts are usually the best, but many of these areas have only sporadic seasons, opening only when the need arises. The best way to find out about these hunts is to constantly monitor areas with high hog populations where hunts have taken place in the past. Most of these opportunities are by drawing only, but you can't draw if you don't apply. So it is best to apply frequently, and at numerous locations, until you're successful.

SCENT CONTROL

A recent, unsuccessful hog hunt gave me a refresher course in the importance of scent elimination and the careful monitoring of air currents. I have touched on the subject throughout this

Tips for Successful Hunting

book, but it deserves special attention here, as so many hunters ignore it and suffer the consequences, often without even knowing it.

For gun hunters, scent control is much easier than it is for hunters carrying a primitive weapon. Hunters who carry weapons capable of cleanly taking a hog from beyond fifty yards should be able to successfully defeat the animal's sensitive nose by simply monitoring wind direction and choosing stand sites or stalking directions accordingly. If the wind shifts at the wrong time, most animals within sight can still be taken before they flee.

In long-range situations, your scent rarely reaches game animals in high concentrations. It's akin to encountering a faint smell of skunk that is somewhere in the distance versus being

A small feather or frayed piece of chenille attached to your gun or bow will help you monitor wind direction.

sprayed at point-blank range. Most hogs don't get too nervous about a light whiff of scent, but give them a full snout of human odor and they'll be gone in a flash.

In some situations, it's simply impossible to control scent enough to get within bow, handgun, or muzzleloader range. This usually means swirling winds. One second a light breeze is hitting you in the face, the next it's pushing ever so slightly at the back of your neck. And you can always count on this to happen at precisely the wrong moment. You have but two options when you notice swirling wind currents: go home (yeah, right!) or maximize scent control, monitor air currents, and cross your fingers for luck.

Maximum scent control is achieved by washing thoroughly with a scent-eliminating soap. Dry with a scent-free towel, and then don clean hunting clothes that have been washed with a scent-free laundry detergent and air dried in the outdoors (this in-

Hunting into the wind and working to eliminate your scent will pay dividends in the field.

cludes any underclothing). For added protection, finish off with a scent-dampening suit like those made by Scent-Lok. And whether or not you choose a suit that adsorbs scent, use a scent-eliminating spray generously on your outer clothing.

Even with all these precautions, though, always remember that it's impossible to entirely eliminate scent, particularly in hot weather. Your goal should be to reduce it enough to gain those few extra yards that often spell the difference between a quick, clean kill and a marginal shot opportunity.

With wild hogs, it only takes one group member to spook before the jig is up. Unlike deer, when one hog takes off, the rest of the group will almost immediately crash through the brush as well.

ACCURACY IS A MUST

Hogs are extremely tough animals. Their skin is not all that thick but it's difficult to penetrate. Their bones are dense and compactly placed and their vitals seem to ride low, and forward, in the chest cavity. Also, in most situations, I have found that they do not bleed heavily when wounded. Any blood trail that does exist is often very hard to follow due to the thick vegetation they prefer. So it's imperative that bullet or arrow placement be perfect, ensuring a quick kill.

Precise shot placement means practicing as much as possible before you head afield. Getting to know your weapon is very important. Most knowledgeable sportsmen pride themselves on their accuracy, and this feeling is only reinforced by consistently putting animals down quickly in a variety of situations.

But it's not enough to just shoot accurately. You must choose proper shot angles and then shoot only when the situation is right. I've taken more than a couple of hogs that had been shot

Shooting an arrow at a leaf or other easily identifiable object is a great way to determine yardage without a rangefinder.

before. While skinning, I've found broadheads—even whole arrows—shotgun pellets, rifle bullets, and muzzleloader projectiles in various parts of the body. We all know that even the most skilled of hunters occasionally hits an animal poorly, but I'd be willing to bet that most of these hogs were the victims of hunters who didn't make good decisions about shot angles and timing. They probably rushed their shots, taking the first shot opportunity instead of the best one.

On one particular hunt in an area reserved for archery hunting, Eric Smith made a solid hit on a hog at about thirty-five yards. At the shot, the large boar turned and made his way straight toward his pursuer. Most hunters in this situation would have stepped aside, but Smith held his ground and at six feet placed a Muzzy-tipped carbon arrow squarely into the skull of the oncoming tusker. (This angle definitely isn't in the preferred-shot category, but in this situation it was a case of take the shot, get a tusk in the leg, or get out of the way.)

3-D archery tournaments are an excellent way to improve accuracy and keep your skills sharp.

Smith noted that, "When I shot it was almost like he had run head-on into a brick wall." Upon skinning and quartering, he found that his first shot was lethal, but it was impossible to be sure in the heat of the moment. Also, another broadhead from a previous hunter was found buried in the shoulder. The hog seemingly suffered no long-term ill effects from the earlier wound—other than a bad attitude toward bowhunters.

The best shots are obviously taken at reasonable distances at standing or slowly moving animals that are broadside or slightly quartering away. These rules certainly apply to gun hunters, but they are etched in stone for bowhunters.

PHYSICAL FITNESS

Depending on your particular location and hunting method, physical fitness can be a major factor in the success in your hunt. Obviously, it doesn't take a lot of effort to climb into a stand and

The Complete Book of Wild Boar Hunting

watch a feeding station. But on the flipside, chasing a pack of aggressive hounds through mountainous or swampy terrain or walking several miles through rolling hill country while spot-and-stalk hunting can really drain you. Making sure you're in good enough shape to hunt all day can spell the difference between success and failure.

I'm certainly not a health professional, but I know that every hunter will benefit from getting in shape before heading into the field. If you don't already stay in good shape year-

Physical fitness was a major key to the success of this group. Each hunter had to walk several miles each day of the hunt.

Tips for Successful Hunting

round, start your training program at least ninety days prior to your planned hunt. Begin with a daily routine of fast walking for at least thirty minutes and work up from there in smooth increments. When it's time to hunt you should be able to chase hogs all day long. And remember, it is much easier to stick to a year-round program than to randomly start and stop these training sessions.

KNOWLEDGE IS POWER

In this modern age of widespread and easily obtainable information, hunters have good access to a lot of helpful information. And as interest in hog hunting is on the rise, new sources of information devoted solely to the sport are beginning to spring up.

Magazines, websites, and videos are all worth looking into. *Boar Hunter* magazine (1–888–297–2627) is one of the most helpful resources. Each issue contains hunting tips and ideas for destinations, as well as stories of the hunt that inform and entertain the reader. Another good idea is to visit one of the prominent Internet search engines and type in "hog hunting" or related terms. You'll be amazed at the wealth of great information that is immediately at your fingertips. You may have to wade through some junk to find the best websites, but it's time well spent if you're a serious hunter.

HUNT AS OFTEN AS POSSIBLE

Hunting as much as possible may sound like a no-brainer to many hunters, but this goes beyond just taking as many hunting trips as possible. It means packing plenty of water and a lunch so you can hunt as long as possible during the day, putting on plenty of miles while scouting, stalking, and hunting, and getting in the field whenever you can.

In certain areas, hogs will move at all hours of the day or night. In more heavily hunted areas, hogs may move only within thirty minutes or an hour of sunrise or sunset. But even when their movements are limited, the hogs have to be somewhere. If you figure out where, you can stay in the field and have productive hunts while everyone else is heading home.

Dog hunters often quit by lunchtime each day, as the majority of hog activity ceases within an hour of daylight. But aggressive hunters will lead their dogs by hand into areas that are certain to contain hogs. Push a resting hog from his bed and the race is on. It takes a little more work to hunt all day, but you'll be well rewarded.

The same goes for stand hunters. Sitting on stand over feeders or natural food sources is a great way to get a crack at an unsuspecting hog, but most stands are only productive very early in the morning and late in the evening. So what do most hunters do in between these times? Take a nap,

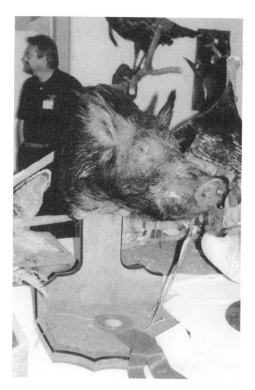

The hunter who spends the most time in the field usually has the best chance of putting a trophy on the wall.

Tips for Successful Hunting

eat a long lunch, catch up on some reading. Put that stuff aside and grab your gear and hit the thickets that you know are likely bedding areas. Work slowly through these areas and you'll be surprised at how many hogs you encounter.

Hunters chasing javelina and warthogs will also enjoy successful hunts during midday, as both species move much more freely than wild hogs during the daylight hours.

Appendix

FINDING PLACES TO HUNT WILD BOAR

Wild hogs can be found in as many as twenty-five to thirty states, give or take, and state game agencies are usually more than glad to provide helpful information to visiting hunters. Also, a growing number of outfitters and lodges are now offering quality hog hunts, and compared to the price of normal big game hunts, these are dirt cheap. A top-of-the-line hog hunt in a premier destination usually runs less than a thousand dollars.

Obviously, the top three hog-hunting destinations are, in no particular order, Florida, Texas, and California. But many other states have high populations in specific areas. For instance, my home state of North Carolina has plenty of hogs, but their distribution is very uneven. They're mostly confined to the western mountains, and hunters typically chase them with dogs because hunting over bait is illegal here. (North Carolina is one of the only states that classifies wild hogs as game animals and regulates their harvest.) The total number of hogs taken by hunters here is fairly small, but the hunting can be great at times. The same is true for many other states.

Appendix

What follows is a compilation of contact information for states that usually have huntable populations of wild hogs. Start doing some research and making some phone calls to state agencies, and you'll soon find more hog hunting that you can do in a lifetime.

STATE AGENCIES

Alabama Division of Wildlife and Freshwater Fisheries
64 N. Union Street, Suite 468
Montgomery, Alabama 36130
www.dcnr.state.Al.us
334-242-3469

Arkansas Game and Fish Commission
2 Natural Resources Drive
Little Rock, AR 72205
www.agfc.state.ar.us/index.html
1-800-364-4263

California Department of Fish and Game
1416 Ninth Street
Sacramento, CA 95814
www.dfg.ca.gov
916-445-0411

Florida Fish and Wildlife Conservation Commission
620 S. Meridian Street
Tallahassee, FL 32399
850-922-4330
www.floridaconservation.org

Appendix

Georgia Department of Natural Resources
2111 US 278 SE
Social Circle, GA 30025
georgiawildlife.dnr.state.ga.us
912-426-5267

Hawaii Department of Land and Natural Resources
1151 Punchbowl Street
Honolulu, HI 96813
www.state.hi.us/dlnr/
808-587-0166

Kentucky Department of Fish and Wildlife
1 Game Farm Road
Frankfort, KY 40601
www.kdfwr.state.ky.us
1-800-858-1549

Louisiana Department of Wildlife and Fisheries
2000 Quail Drive
Baton Rouge, LA 70898
www.wlf.state.la.us
225-765-2925

Maryland Department of Natural Resources
580 Taylor Avenue
Wildlife & Heritage Division
Annapolis, MD 21401
www.dnr.state.md.us
410-260-8540

Maine Department of Inland Fisheries and Wildlife
41 State House Station
284 State Street
Augusta, ME 04333
www.state.me.us/ifw/homepage.htm
207-287-8000

Massachusetts Division of Fisheries and Wildlife
251 Causeway Street
Suite 400
Boston, MA 02114
www.state.ma.us/dfwele/dfw/dfw_toc.htm
617-626-1590

Mississippi Department of Wildlife, Fisheries and Parks
1505 Eastover Drive
Jackson, MS 39211
www.mdwfp.com
601-432-2400

Missouri Department of Conservation
2901 W. Truman Boulevard
P.O. Box 180
Jefferson City, MO 65109
www.conservation.state.mo.us/
573-751-4115

Nebraska Game and Parks Commission
2200 N. 33rd Street
Lincoln, NE 68503
www.ngpc.state.ne.us/homepage.html
402-471-0641

Appendix

New Hampshire Fish and Game Department
Public Affairs Division
11 Hazen Drive
Concord, NH 03301
www.wildlife.state.nh.us
603-271-3211

New Jersey Division of Fish and Wildlife
P.O. Box 400
Trenton, NJ 08625
www.state.nj.us/dep/fgw
609-292-2965

New Mexico Department of Game and Fish
P.O. Box 25112
Santa Fe, NM 87507
www.wildlife.state.nm.us
1-800-862-9310

New York Division of Fish, Wildlife and Marine Resources
625 Broadway
Albany, NY 12233
www.dec.state.ny.us/website/dfwmc
518-402-8919

North Carolina Wildlife Resources Commission
1722 Mail Service Center
Division of Wildlife Management
Raleigh, NC 27699
www.ncwildlife.org
919-733-7291

Ohio Division of Wildlife
1840 Belcher Drive
Columbus, OH 43224
www.dnr.state.oh.us/wildlife/default.htm
1-800-945-3543

Oklahoma Department of Wildlife and Conservation
P.O. Box 53465
Wildlife Division
Oklahoma City, OK 73152
www.wildlifedepartment.com
405-521-2739

Pennsylvania Department of Conservation
and Natural Resources
2001 Elmerton Avenue
Harrisburg, PA 17110
www.dcnr.state.pa.us
717-787-4250

South Carolina Division of Natural Resources
Rembert C. Dennis Building
P.O. Box 167
Game and Fish Department
Columbia, SC 29202
www.dnr.state.sc.us/
803-734-3886

Appendix

Tennessee Wildlife Resources Agency
Ellington Agricultural Center
P.O. Box 40747
Nashville, TN 37204
www.state.tn.us/twra
615-781-6610

Texas Parks and Wildlife Department
4200 Smith School Road
Austin, TX 78744
www.tpwd.state.tx.us
1-800-792-1112 or 512-389-4800

Vermont Agency of Natural Resources
103 S. Main Street
Waterbury, VT 05671
www.anr.state.vt.us
802-241-3700

Index

A
Accessing quality property, 183–186
Accuracy, 189–191
Africa
   warthogs, 149
Aging sign, 45
Alabama
   hunting areas, 15
   state wildlife agency websites, addresses, phone numbers, 198
Alligators
   photograph, 74
Aluminum shafts, 60
Archery equipment, 59–61
   size, 60
Archery tournaments
   3-D, 191
Argentina
   huntable hog population, 124
   spot and stalk hunting, 126
Arizona
   javelina, 132
Arkansas
   state wildlife agency websites, addresses, phone numbers, 198
Armadillos
   photograph, 105
Arrows, 61
   aluminum shafts, 60
   open-on-contact (mechanical) broadhead, 60
   shafts, 60
Attractants, 64
Australia
   huntable hog population, 124
   hunting with dogs, 126
   outfitters list, 127–128

B
Bag limits, 15–16
Bait hunting
   bait replenishing, 24
   baits preferred, 24
   distribution options, 24
   hot weather, 81–82
   methods, 21–27
      photograph, 22, 23, 25
   prohibited in California, 102
   Texas, 106
Barbecued ribs
   recipe, 166
Barnes X-Bullet, 56
Basic commands
   for dog training, 39

Bays, 38
Bedding areas, 52–53, 134
  photograph, 46, 52
Binoculars, 69–71
  California, 71
  photograph, 70
  southeast, 69–70
Black Beard's Island, 3
  photograph, 2
Black River Plantation, 87
Black River Swamp, 87
Blinds
  photograph, 29
  requirements, 29
Bloodlines
  originated, 9
Bluetick
  hunting hounds, 36
Boars. *See* Hogs
Boot blankets, 68
Bowhunter
  and practice, 63
Bow hunting
  personal experiences, 4–6
Breathable clothing, 64
Broadhead, 60, 61
Bug-Out Outdoorwear, Inc., 78
Bugs, 77–79
Bug spray, 64
Bullet design, 56
Butchering, 157–159

C
Calibers used, 57
California
  baiting
    prohibited, 102
  binoculars, 71
  guides, 101
  hogs
    hunting classification, 100
    photograph, 100, 101, 124
  hunting, 99–102, 197
  hunting areas, 15
  hunting methods, 101–102
    spot and stalk hunting, 101–102
  nonresident hunters, 100
  spotting scopes, 71
  state wildlife agency
    websites, addresses, phone numbers, 198
  tag cost, 100
  trophy quality and populations, 102
Canada
  huntable hog population, 124
  outfitters list, 128
Canned hunts, 110
Canning, 167–169
Carbon shafts, 60
Cartridges
  for short-range hunting, 56
Catch dogs. *See also* Hounds
  photograph, 4
  using, 3–7
Centerfire rifles, 56
Chaps, 64
Citric acid
  purpose, 85
Close encounter

Index

with wild hogs, 1–2
Clothing, 65–68
  breathable, 64
  cold-weather, 64
  Gore-Tex, 64
  northeast, 67–68
  protecting from elements, 64
  southeast, 65–66
  southwest, 66–67
  summer hunting, 79–80
Cold-weather clothing, 64
Coleman fuel, 180
Collared peccary, 131–143
Compasses, 72
Compound bows
  photograph, 60
Cooking process, 164–166
Cookout, 164–165
Cooling
  hot-weather hunt, 84
  process, 159
Cottonmouth
  South Carolina, 74
Cumberland Mountains of Tennessee, 13
Cut-on-contact broadhead, 61

D
Deer
  photograph, 82
Degreasers, 180
De Soto, Hernando, 10
Disease, 16–18
Dog. *See also* Hounds
  handling
    experiences, 5–7
  training, 39–41
    basic commands, 39
    beginning age, 39
    voice commands, 39
Dog hunters, 194
Domestic hogs, 12
Double Bull
  photograph, 29
Double Bull Archery blinds, 30

E
Equipment
  needed, 1–2, 55–72
  protecting from elements, 64
Eurasian bloodline, 9
Europe
  outfitters list, 129
European mount, 178–179

F
Facemask, 68
Feeders
  do-it-yourselfer, 25–26
Feeding areas
  photograph, 46
Feeding stations
  photograph, 23
Feral, 9
Feral hogs. *See also* Hogs
  found, 10
  photograph, 11
Field-care problems, 173
Field dressing, 84, 157–159

Findings and interpreting signs, 43–53
Fixed-power scope, 71
Florida
  hunting, 91, 197
    areas, 15
    opportunities, 96
    state wildlife agency websites, addresses, phone numbers, 198
Food sources, 44
Footwear, 65–68
  northeast, 67–68
  southeast, 65–66
  southwest, 66–67
Free-roam farming, 11
Full-sized binoculars, 70–71

G
Game biologists
  resources, 184
Game care
  hot-weather, 83–85
Game cart
  photograph, 64
Game Tracker, 84
Generic sausage mixes, 162
Georgia
  hog classification, 94
  hunting
    areas, 15
    opportunities, 96
  state wildlife agency websites, addresses, phone numbers, 199
Glassing, 71

Global positioning systems (GPS), 64, 72
Glo-mitts, 68
Gore-Tex clothing, 64
Government .45–.70, 56
Grilling out, 164–165
Guides
  after wild hogs, 94–95
  California, 101

H
Habitat
  photograph, 34
Half mounts, 176–178
Handguns
  photograph, 58
  size, 58, 59
Hawaii
  hunting, 106–107
    areas, 15
  state wildlife agency websites, addresses, phone numbers, 199
Hawaiian Islands, 10
Head skinning, 175
Hide
  no refrigeration available, 175
  preserving, 174
Hog(s), 9–19
  behavior, 14
  classification by states, 94
  color, 12
  found, 10
  ideal cooking temperature, 165

Index

photograph, 3, 8, 10, 11, 13, 32, 57, 58, 80, 93, 101, 103, 126
  with piglets, 17
  trails, 46
population
  southeastern states, 96–97
preferred foods, 44
preferred habitat, 44
quality of meat, 158
roast, 164–165
roasting recipe, 164
sense of smell
  examples, 32–33
southern, 87–97
taped sounds, 36
types of mounts, 171
unpredictable movement, 82
Homemade feeders, 25–26
Homemade sausage
  making, 161
Hood-rig, 38
Hood rigging, 4
Hot weather hunting, 80–83
  game care, 83–85
  over bait, 81–82
  patience, 81–82
  skinning and cooling, 84
  still method, 82–83
Hounds
  beneficial for
    locating wounded, 40
  breeds, 36
  handling
    experiences, 5–7
  photograph, 4
  training, 39–41
  using, 3–7
Hunters
  caliber size used, 57
Hunting
  around the world, 123–129
  destinations
    choosing, 183
    top three, 197
  from field to table, 157–169
  finding places, 197–203
  first experience, 109–113
  Florida, 91
  Hawaii, 106–107
  in hot weather, 80–83
  with hounds, 3–7, 36, 93
  javelina, 138–142
  methods, 21–41
    calling, 34–36
    with hounds, 36
    over bait, 21–27
    personal experiences, 22–23
    stalking and still hunting, 30–33
    stand hunting, 27–30
    stand *vs.* blind, 28–30
  often, 193–195
  opportunities, 96
  outfitters around the world, 127–128
  personal experience, 1–7
  preserves, 109–121
  pressure, 183
  public property, 185
  South Carolina, 90

Hunting, methods (*continued*)
   southeast, 90, 92–93
   success, 43
   tactics, 92–93, 126
   tips for successful, 183–195
   warthogs, 151–153
   into wind, 188
   year-round, 73–85

I
Insulated boots, 64

J
Javelina, 131–143
   breeding, 136
   calling, 141–142
   differentiating between
      genders, 142–143
   feeding
      sign, 135
   food, 134–136
   glassing, 139–140
   habits, 133–134
   hunter success rate, 131
   hunting tactics, 138–142
   lifespan, 137–138
   population, 132, 137, 139
      in Southwest, 131
   range and distribution, 132
   sign, 134
   size, 136
   spot and stalk hunting,
      139–140
   still hunting, 140–141
   trophy hunting, 142–143

   water, 134–136
      needs, 135
      and wild hog, 132

K
Kentucky
   state wildlife agency
      websites, addresses,
         phone numbers, 199
Knight .52-caliber
   muzzleloader, 89
Knowledge, 193

L
Laser rangefinder
   photograph, 69
Layering, 68
Life-sized mounts, 176–178
Limited-entry public lands
   hunting, 186
Little Ugly, 152
Loads for shotguns, 57–58
Longbow, 60
Louisiana
   hog-hunting opportunities,
      96
   state wildlife agency
      websites, addresses,
         phone numbers, 199
Lyme disease (ticks), 78

M
Magnum Fifty-Five-Gallon
   Tripod Feeder, 24–25
Maine

Index

state wildlife agency
  websites, addresses,
    phone numbers, 200
Marlin .450, 56
Maryland
  state wildlife agency
    websites, addresses,
      phone numbers, 199
Massachusetts
  state wildlife agency
    websites, addresses,
      phone numbers, 200
Mathews Q2XL, 61
Meat
  ideal cooking temperature, 165
  marinate or soak, 159–161
  preparation, 159–161
  preserving, 174
  roasting recipe, 164
  storing technique, 160–161
Mechanical broadhead, 60
Merino sheep, 110
Mexico
  huntable hog population, 124
  outfitters list, 128
Mississippi
  state wildlife agency
    websites, addresses,
      phone numbers, 200
Missouri
  state wildlife agency
    websites, addresses,
      phone numbers, 200

Moisture-wicking garments, 79
Mosquitoes, 78
Moultrie Feeders, 24–25
Mount
  choosing, 175–182
Mountain cur
  hunting hounds, 36
Muzzleloaders, 57
  Knight .52-caliber, 89
Muzzy broadhead, 60
  photograph, 61
Muzzy 115-grain, 60

N
Natural foods, 27–28
Nebraska
  state wildlife agency
    websites, addresses,
      phone numbers, 200
New Hampshire
  Russian boar population, 16
  state wildlife agency
    websites, addresses,
      phone numbers, 201
New Jersey
  state wildlife agency
    websites, addresses,
      phone numbers, 201
New Mexico
  javelina, 132
  state wildlife agency
    websites, addresses,
      phone numbers, 201
New York
  state wildlife agency

New York (*continued*)
    websites, addresses, phone numbers, 201
New Zealand
    huntable hog population, 124
    hunting with dogs, 126
    outfitters list, 127–128
Nikon products, 68
North Carolina
    hog classification, 94
    hunting, 197
        with dogs, 93
    Russian boar population, 16
    state wildlife agency websites, addresses, phone numbers, 201
Northeast
    clothing and footwear, 67–68

O

Oaks
    food for hogs, 28
    photograph, 28
Ohio
    state wildlife agency websites, addresses, phone numbers, 202
Oklahoma
    hunting areas, 15
    state wildlife agency websites, addresses, phone numbers, 202
    wild hogs
        photograph, 107
Open-on-contact (mechanical) broadhead, 60
Optics, 68–72
Outfitters
    after wild hogs, 94–95
    around the world, 127–128

P

Patience
    hot weather, 81–82
Pen hunts, 113
Pennsylvania
    state wildlife agency websites, addresses, phone numbers, 202
Physical fitness, 191–193
Piglets, 15
Pig pickin', 164–165
Pipe feeders, 26–27
    size, 26
Plott hunting hounds, 36
Polynesians, 10
Pork pull, 164–165
Portable blinds, 29–30
Porter, Ron, 152–153
Practicing, 189
Preserve hunting, 109–121
    advantages, 118
    inquiry questions, 114–120
    methods, 119
    photograph, 116
    pricing guidelines, 118
    purpose, 118
Pressure cookers, 168
Private property

Index

hunting, 185
Pseudorabies, 17
Public property
   hunting, 185
Pygmy hog, 123

R
Rangefinder
   photograph, 69
Razorback Russian-looking
      hog, 109
Recurve, 60
Redbone hunting hounds, 36
Remington .35, 56
Remington magnum, 56
Rifle calibers
   suggested, 56
Rifle scopes, 71
Rocky Mountain, 61
Rooting, 48–49
   signs
      photograph, 48
Roundups, 11
Rubs, 50–51
   photograph, 51
   reason for, 51
Rug, 176–178
   cut, 178
   photograph, 176
Russia
   huntable hog population, 124
Russian boars, 9, 12. *See also* Hogs
   characteristics, 13–15

photograph, 13

S
Sahara
   warthogs, 149
Sal Soda, 179
Sausage, 161–164
   making, 161, 163
   recipe, 163–164
Scat, 47–48, 134
   photograph, 47
Scent control, 186–189
Scent-eliminating system, 79
Scent eliminators, 64
Scopes, 71
Scouting, 24, 27, 28, 43–53, 194
   javelina, 134
   trails, 47
   when, 52–53
Scratching posts, 51
Season, 15–16
Sense of smell
   examples, 32–33
Shoats, 14
Shot angles and placement, 56, 62–64, 189
   and timing
      making good decisions, 190
Shotguns
   10-gauge, 57
   12-gauge, 57
   loads for, 57–58
   in South, 57

Shoulder mount, 175–176
Sign, 134
Skinning
   conventional or rug, 177–178
   hot-weather hunt, 84
   for life-sized mounts,
      176–177
   no refrigeration available,
      175
Skull(s)
   bleaching process, 181
   degrease, 180
   photograph, 179
Skull mount (European),
   178–179
Smith, Eric, 190–191
Snake(s), 73–77
   protection from, 76
   tips for avoiding, 75–76
   venom
      purposes, 75
Snakebite victims, 76
Snakeproof boots, 64, 76
   photograph, 77
Snuffer, 61
South
   shotguns, 57
South America
   javelina, 132
   outfitters list, 129
   spot and stalk hunting, 126
South Carolina
   hog classification, 94
   hunting, 90
      areas, 15
      with dogs, 93

   opportunities, 96
   lowlands, 3, 87
   state wildlife agency
      websites, addresses,
         phone numbers, 202
   water moccasin
      (cottonmouth), 74
Southeast
   binoculars, 69–70
   clothing and footwear, 65–66
   finding hogs, 95–97
   hog country
      photograph, 92
   hunting, 90
      with dogs, 93
      tactics, 92–93
   state hog population, 96–97
Southern-fried pork chops
   recipe, 166–167
Southern hogs, 87–97
Southwest
   clothing and footwear, 66–67
   spotting scopes, 71
Sow
   photograph, 89
Spotting scopes, 71–72
Stand hunting, 194
   in hot weather, 80–82
State agencies
   websites, addresses, phone
      numbers, 198
States
   hog classification, 94
Still hunting
   hot weather, 82–83
   personal experiences, 31–32

success rates, 83
  tips, 33
Strike dogs, 37
Stroff, Mike, 87
Suidae scrofa, 123
Summer hunting
  clothing, 79–80
Swamp buggy
  photograph, 91
Swamp hog hunting, 88
Swift A-Frame, 56
Swine brucellosis, 17

T
Teeth wear
  aging, 138
Tennessee
  Cumberland Mountains, 13
  hunting with dogs, 93, 114
  state wildlife agency
    websites, addresses,
      phone numbers, 203
Texas
  hogs
    photograph, 104, 105, 106
  hunting, 99, 103–105, 197
    areas, 15
    methods, 104–105
  javelina, 132
  Russian boar population, 16
  state wildlife agency
    websites, addresses,
      phone numbers, 203
ThermaCell, 79
Three-blade Muzzy broadhead
  photograph, 61

3-D archery tournaments, 191
Thunderhead, 61
Ticks, 78
Timed feeders, 24, 25
Tracks, 45–47, 134
Trails, 45–47
Trophy, 19
  and bacteria, 174
  field-care basics, 172–174
  preparation, 171–182
  proper field dressing
    photograph, 173
  status, 18–19
Trophy Bonded Bear Claw, 56
Tusks
  male *vs.* female, 18
  photograph, 19, 62, 146, 148
  size vs. age, 18

V
Variable scopes, 71
Vermont
  state wildlife agency
    websites, addresses,
      phone numbers, 203
Viper, 75
Visayan warty hog, 123

W
Wallows, 49–50
  photograph, 49, 50
Warthogs, 145–155
  Africa, 154–155
  characteristics, 146–151
  choosing outfitter, 154–155
  fighting, 147–149

Warthogs (*continued*)
  habits, 146–151
  hunting, 151–153
  lifespan, 151
  location, 149
  mating season, 150
  meal, 154
  photograph, 148
    habitats, 150
    trophy caliber, 146
  recommended weapons, 153–154
  size, 147
  traveling patterns, 149
Wasp 100- or 125-grain models, 61
Water moccasin (cottonmouth) South Carolina, 74
Weapons for hogs, 55–61
Western hogs, 99–107
  photograph, 103
West Nile virus (Mosquitoes), 78
Whitening process, 180
Whitening product, 181
Wild boar, 9–19. *See also* Hog(s)
  size, 13–14
Wild hogs. *See also* Hog(s)
  color, 12
  photograph, 12, 31, 56, 160
Wildlife enforcement officers
  resources, 184
Wild turkey
  photograph, 94
Winchester .300, 56
Winchester's FailSafe, 56
Wind direction
  monitoring, 187
Woodsman skills, 43

Y

Year-round hunting, 73–85

Z

Zwickey, 61